CW00666517

A VIEW OF CHINA

A VIEW OF CHINA

Dora Gauss

The Book Guild Ltd
Sussex, England

The Book Guild Ltd.
25 High Street,
Lewes, Sussex

First published 1999

Set in Times
Typesetting by
Acorn Bookwork, Salisbury, Wiltshire

Printed in Great Britain by
Bookcraft (Bath) Ltd, Avon

A catalogue record for this book is
available from the British Library

ISBN 1 85776 415 3

CONTENTS

ACKNOWLEDGEMENTS

I would like to express my gratitude to the many students, (Extra-Mural, WEA, VIth form, as well as school pupils), who have made my life as a geographer so happy and worthwhile, and also to the members of my family who have helped so much with getting the book into print: my elder daughter Judith, my son John and my husband Hubert without whose patience and co-operation the book could not have been written.

INTRODUCTION

There must surely be as many views of China as there are viewers: hence the title of this book,

China is one of the oldest and largest countries in the world. With a history of over 5,000 years, and a population exceeding 1,000 million, it forms one of the largest sections of the human race and bids fair to take its place as one of the great powers of the future.

This book is the result of a love affair with that country lasting almost a lifetime. It began in the author's childhood, when a friend of her father from his student days paid frequent visits to the family when on leave from his work as a civil engineer helping to build the modern roads and railways of China. His work took him to Sichuan, the beautiful province in Western China sometimes called 'The Paradise on Earth' on account of its equable climate and fertile soil. The size of France, it now has a population of 100 million, larger than that of Japan.

For many years Walter Shipway, the civil engineer mentioned, travelled up and down the rapids of the middle Yangtze River (now the Changjiang) in the region of the Three Gorges on junks hauled by trackers slithering along the rocky banks harnessed to ropes of bamboo fibre. On one occasion his luggage was stolen by bandits, and he insisted against all advice on visiting their cave to demand its restoration. They were so amazed by his courage that they handed it back!

The middle Yangtze, with its Three Gorges, became one of the chief river journeys of the world, and fortunate indeed are those who made it before that wonderful scene disappeared beneath the waters of the great dam (San Xia or Three Gorges), which, if it fulfils the dream of its planners, will make

China one of the foremost producers of hydroelectric power on earth. It is to be hoped that not too great a price has been paid in terms of loss of scenery and ancient towns and cities, the sacrifice of agricultural land and the compulsory migration of millions of people.

My view of China is bound to be coloured by geography. What does that mean? As far as possible it will be an overall view, including everything that covers the physical environment and Man's response to it, not only in farming, but in lifestyle, including the response of art, literature and crafts such as silk and porcelain and, in ancient times, bronze. This analysis can never be completed as it changes with time, but it forms a fascinating study, and can only improve international understanding. To give a crude example, the life of an Eskimo vis-à vis that of a peasant in Sichuan and the basic contrast is very clear: each has made the best of his particular environment.

The author hopes that readers will enjoy the book and be encouraged to read further, and better still, to visit that wonderful country, or make some contact with overseas Chinese. When I decided to write the book, as a result of suggestions by my students, I gave up lecturing and set out a plan of study and travel. As far as possible I visited all the main areas of China, and filled in as many gaps as I could with reading, including the good translations from the Chinese, especially poetry, much of which comes through as delightful in English as it must be in Chinese.

As a teenager, I had been warned by Walter Shipway not to attempt the study of the language unless I was prepared to give my whole life to it. It was clear that geography would be my life's work, and being a woman, and hoping for children, I could not involve myself beyond a certain point.

In the 1970s I found myself sitting next to an elderly Chinese and his wife on a coach tour of Exeter connected with a conference of the British Society of Friends (Quakers) who had invited them to England. He was a retired doctor who had received his medical training from English Quakers many years ago. He told me he lived in Chengdu in Sichuan and I mentioned Walter Shipway to him. To my amazement and delight he said, 'I knew him when I was a boy. He helped the Quakers to run a boys' club in Chongqing to which I belonged.' We talked a lot and he said, 'You will always find a friend in Chengdu.' I visited Chengdu in 1989 and met him again. Unfortunately we were unable to visit his home owing to the illness of his wife who died later. We left China on the Sunday before the tragedy in Tiananmen Square.

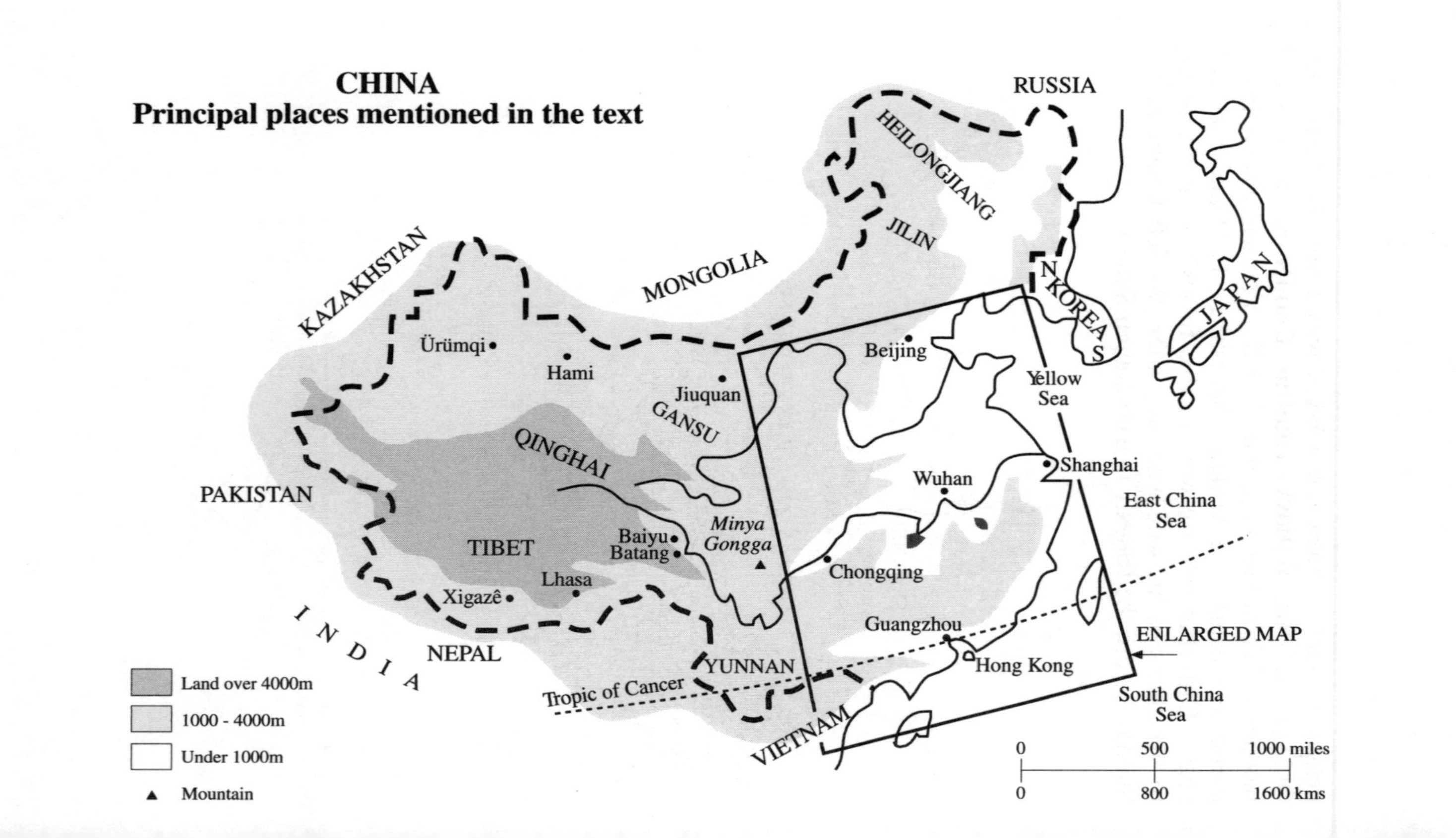
CHINA
Principal places mentioned in the text
RUSSIA
HEILONGJIANG
JILIN
KAZAKHSTAN
MONGOLIA
N KOREA S
JAPAN
Ürümqi
Hami
Jiuquan
GANSU
Beijing
Yellow Sea
QINGHAI
Shanghai
Wuhan
East China Sea
PAKISTAN
TIBET
Baiyu
Batang
Minya Gongga
Chongqing
Lhasa
Xigazê
INDIA
NEPAL
YUNNAN
Guangzhou
Hong Kong
ENLARGED MAP
Tropic of Cancer
VIETNAM
South China Sea
Land over 4000m
1000 - 4000m
Under 1000m
Mountain
0
500
1000 miles
0
800
1600 kms

EASTERN CHINA
Principal places mentioned in the text

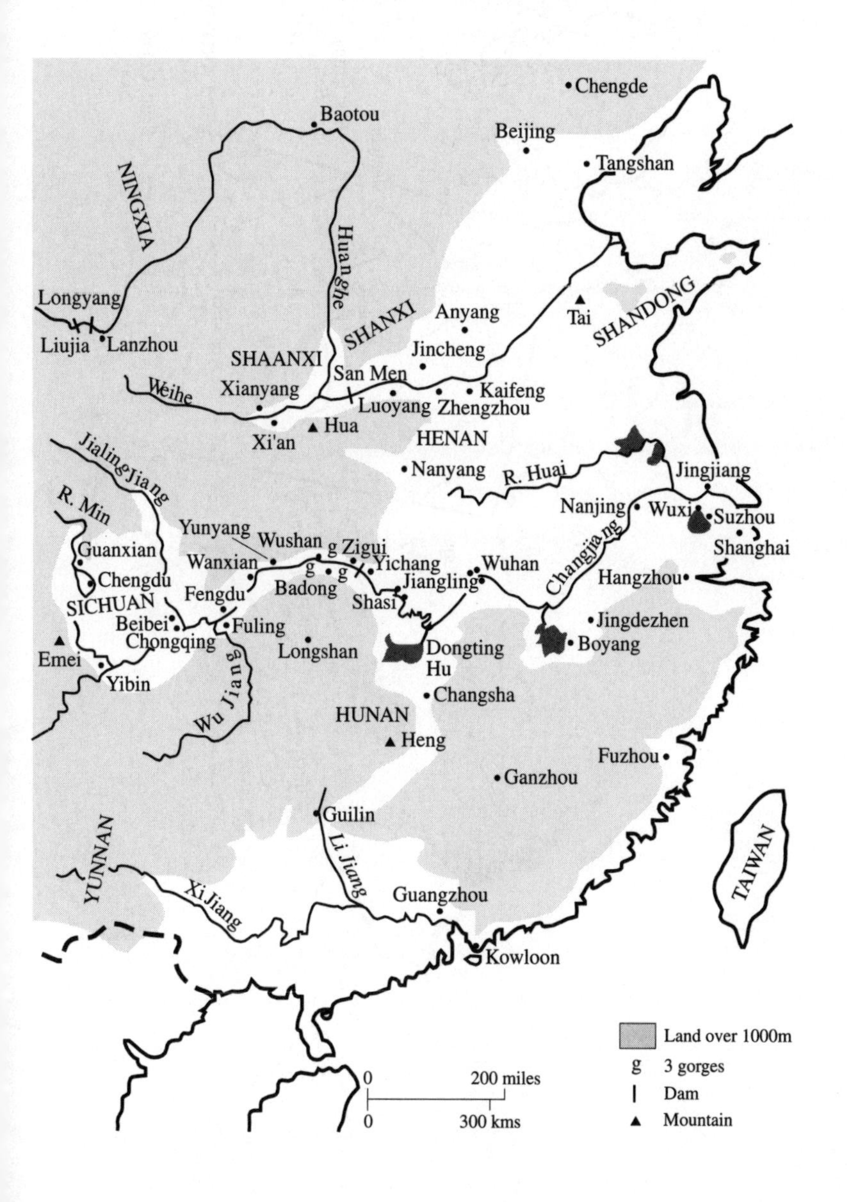

1

THE YELLOW EARTH AND THE YELLOW RIVER

On the north side of Tiananmen square in Beijing, to the west of the main gate into the Forbidden City, is the entrance to an interesting little park seldom visited by tourists, the Zhongshan Park. Here is the Altar of Earth and Grain, a link with ancient China. It was the custom for two special enclosures to be built adjoining a ruler's palace, to the east an ancestral shrine containing family records, and on the west a mound and tree, the Altar of Soil, representing the land ruled.[1]

The present Altar of Earth and Grain dates from 1421, during the Ming dynasty, when most of the present Palace City was constructed. The Imperial Ancestral Shrine, which lies to the east of Tiananmen Gate, is now a Cultural Park. Both these parks contain some splendid thousand-year-old cypress trees. The Altar of Earth and Grain is a surprise to the Western visitor, as it covers an area of 3000m^2, nearly half the size of a soccer field. It consists of a larger square representing the earth surrounded by four low walls of glazed brick: black for the north, gold for the south, blue for the east, and yellow for the west. Within this is a smaller square, divided into five compartments, each filled with soil from one of the main areas of China: black soil from the prairie-type lands of Heilongjiang and Jilin (formerly Manchuria), white from the desert areas of

[1]Laurence Sickman and Alexander Soper, *The Art and Architecture of China*, (Pelican History of Art), Harmondsworth: Penguin, 1971, p368.

the west, red from the south and grey from the east, representing the newer alluvial soils derived from river silt. In the centre, emphasizing its traditional importance, the smallest square is filled with the famous yellow earth (Huangtu), the fertile soil where Chinese civilization was born, in the Yellow River (Huanghe) valley and on the Great Plain.

The Emperor performed sacrifices twice a year at the Altar. On the north side is a handsome building, once a Hall of Prayer, now a memorial to Sun Yat-Sen, leader of the Revolution of 1911, which led to the founding of the Republic of China.

Today the five colours are clearly discernible though somewhat blurred at the edges and apparently trampled. The rest of the park is pleasantly laid out with trees and flowers and in the south-west corner is a kindergarten from which colourful 'crocodiles' of small children emerge with their teachers to play games of 'Catch the Dragon's tail' and walk round the gardens. The little park is a delightful oasis from the bustle of Chang'an Avenue. Old men perform their Taijiquan exercises under the ancient trees. Babies in bamboo prams and toddlers are everywhere, accompanied by grandparents, or young fathers on their rotation day off.

The yellow earth, so vital to the early development of Chinese civilization was named 'loess' by the 19th-century German geologist, Richthofen. During the final episode of the last Ice Age as the Siberian ice sheet retreated, melting northwards, dry bitter winds carried the fine dust from the moraines to north China, where it was deposited in the valleys and banked against the hills. It covers an area of more than 631,000km^2 and is sometimes as much as 120m deep. The scanty rainfall of north China, occurring mainly in June, July and August, causes severe gullying, and immense quantities of the loess are carried away each year by the Yellow River, which has created the Great Plain. The bed of the river has been built up above the level of the surrounding plain, and over the centuries the breaking of banks has led to floods and many changes of course, leading to disastrous loss of life. Hence the nickname 'China's Sorrow'. Finally the great river enters the Gulf of Bohai.

The loess soil is as fine as talcum powder, but the structure is such that it holds together very well and unless eroded, forms steep vertical cliffs. For centuries, the people have cut cave dwellings into the steep slopes, or the vertical sides of excavated pits. These dwellings were warm in winter and cool in summer, a great advantage in the extreme climate. The walls were plastered, and the cave opening often filled in with a finely carved wooden entrance with a door and paper windows. Nowadays many of these dwellings are used only for storage, though in exposed places people still choose to live in them, rather than in the houses of loess bricks. Indoors the problem of the bitter winter was solved by the 'kang', a box-like brick structure taking up most of the room space. Inside it, a fire of twigs and straw heated the bricks which stored the heat as in our modern off-peak electric heaters or ancient Roman central heating: a chimney took the smoke through an outside wall. The top of the kang served as a comfortable bed for the entire family at night, and for rest and seating during the day.

The soft firm soil is easy to work, but the tendency to gullying has necessitated the building of terraces supported by stone walls – a sentence of hard labour for all concerned! Sometimes crops can be seen above the dwellings with ventilation shafts scattered among the vegetables. Man has settled in this part of China from the earliest times, and archaeology has revealed that this area was indeed the cradle of Chinese civilization. The best soils occur where loess has been mixed with alluvium, along the Weihe valley and on the western side of the Great Plain.

The climate in Neolithic times (4000–1700 BC) was probably warmer and more humid than at present and settlement began on slightly higher ground above the marshy valley floors. An example of a well-documented excavation is the Neolithic village of Banpo, north of Xi'an, which was discovered in the mid 1950s. In 1961 the entire site was roofed in, and a wooden walkway enables visitors to explore the details. A ditch about 10m deep surrounds the settlement, and the houses were grouped round an open space containing a communal building. The burial ground is outside the village on the north side, and on the east is a potters' area with six kilns. The population was 400–600 and the site was occupied, probably in two phases, for about 1000 years (4000–3000 BC). Houses were of several types, the earlier ones round or square, the roofs supported by wooden poles, covered with thatch or beams, and the walls of wattle and daub: still others were built entirely of clay in a wigwam shape, with the entrance above ground level. Later dwellings were rectangular. Storage pits were dug near the houses. Agriculture appears to have been carried on by the women. Evidence of millet and cabbage has been found, and pigs and dogs were reared. Spindle whorls, bone hair-pins and needles, and imprints on the base of pottery, show evidence of basket work, and fabric weaving, possibly of hemp. The men were engaged in hunting and fishing, the latter being particularly important.

In addition to bone harpoons and arrow heads, stone balls strung together with string have been found. Interestingly, these resemble the bolas used by the Patagonian Indians and later adopted by the gauchos, the cattlemen of Argentina: yet another fascinating link between eastern Asia and the Americas via the Bering Strait, along with blowpipes and the use of knotted string by the Incas. It is, however, the pottery unearthed here which has aroused the greatest interest. There is no evidence of the use of the potters' wheel, but coiled pots of great variety were made for cooking and storage and included a two-handled tapered amphora which was let down on strings to bring water up the steep cliffs of loess, and special containers used as coffins for infants who were buried in the floors of the houses. Pots for ordinary use were decorated with pricking or finger-nail marks, but better quality ware was painted in red, black and white with designs of stylized fish and deer, and, in two examples, with a circular mask or representation of a human face. These show a feeling for shape and decoration which presages the long tradition of excellence in the craftsmanship of the Chinese potters. The culture has become known by the name 'Painted Pottery' or Yangshao, after the site east of Banpo where it was first discovered.

Further east at Longshan in Shandong province, specimens

of the now famous Black Pottery came to light in 1928. They are thought to date from the third millennium BC, 1000 years later than the Painted Pottery. In addition to a variety of material for everyday use, the finds included objects probably intended for ritual or purely decorative purposes in a variety of shapes, made from fragile paper-thin material, burnished black, with a fine lustre. There have been endless discussions among experts as to how this was achieved.

During recent years a Chinese sculptor[2] Qiu Zhihai, who became interested in Black Pottery in 1977, has worked tirelessly with his artist son to discover the lost process. From inspection of over 200 ancient kilns he was able to deduce the temperatures (900–1000°C). It appears that the pottery was fired for a very long time in a hot kiln, and then smoked as the kiln cooled, when the black colour was achieved by charcoal grains filling tiny holes in the paste. This had been realized but no one had tried it until Qiu Zhihai and his son renovated an ancient kiln, and finally lit the fire. They lived on the spot for several months, and Qiu controlled the temperature. It took four years and hundreds of experiments before they succeeded. Now they have produced more than 500 pieces, including copies of ancient designs as well as modern creations.

In 1989 Qiu Zhihai was awarded the First Class Scientific and Technological Progress Prize by China's Ministry of Culture and a gold medal at the 28th Brussels Eureka World Invention Fair for his success in recovering the tradition of an art lost for 4000 years. He has held exhibitions in Japan, Taiwan, USSR, Beijing, Singapore and Hong Kong, and hopes to show his work in the USA, Britain and France.

Among many other clues to China's ancient past found in the loess area are the 'oracle bones' dug up in hundreds by peasants in the 19th century and sold to pharmacists to be ground and made into medicinal products. Known to the populace as 'dragon bones' they were marked with what were thought to be magic symbols, but were in fact divination signs,

---

[2] *China Today*, December 1990, Vol XXXIX No 12, p63.

throwing considerable light on the most ancient form of some of the most well known characters in Chinese script. One pit, near Anyang, the capital of the Shang dynasty (14th–11th centuries BC) yielded 18,000 examples. The shoulder blades of cattle and the carapaces of tortoises were in most frequent use. In the *Book of Songs* (the poem refers to a legendary time in the Shang dynasty) we read:

> ... Tan-fu the duke
> At coming of day galloped his horses,
> Going west along the river bank
> Till he came to the foot of Mount Ch'i.
> Where with the lady Chiang
> He came to look for a home.
>
> The plain of Chou was very fertile,
> Its celery and sowthistle sweet as rice-cakes.
> 'Here we will make a start;
> Here take counsel,
> Here notch our tortoise'.
> It says, 'Stop', it says, 'Halt,
> Build houses here.'[3]

The method of divination was as follows: shallow indentations were cut in the concave side of the bone, and hot points were applied to these indentations. This cracked the bone and the angle formed between two cracks gave the answer to the questions asked: these concerned rain, the sowing and harvesting of crops, choice of animals for sacrifices to ancestors, and the most propitious day (of the 10 day week) for the offering. All questions expected the answer 'Yes' or 'No', for example: 'Rain, or not?' 'Reap, or not?' The marks on the oracle bones are clearly a form of picture writing, but over the centuries the characters developed far beyond this stage, to the

---

[3]*Book of Songs*, trans. Arthur Waley, London: George Allen and Unwin, 1969, p248.

point where they became a tool for written communication of all kinds, including during the Tang dynasty some of the finest poetry ever written. The phonetic element added to the characters has ceased to be a guide to pronunciation which has changed greatly with the passage of time.

An eminent scholar of the Chinese language, Arthur Cooper[4], translator of the poetry of Li Bai and Du Fu in the Penguin Classics series, suggested in 1978 that the origin of the Chinese script is connected with a sort of poetic perception of shared experience translated into symbols, which is common to mankind everywhere, and is expressed in metaphors found in languages all over the world. He describes how a particular symbol, two stalks of millet held in a hand, is included in characters representing, for example, hamster, harvest, sickle, spoonbill, humble, corner, screen or curtain. All are connected with harvesting or gleaning: the 'corner' and the 'screen' with the custom of not reaping the corner of the field, which was left for the poor (humble), as in other parts of the world (for example Leviticus, chapter 23, verse 22). The spoonbill and the hamster are well known as gleaners. 'Corner' is also a metaphor for the corner of a room, which may be 'screened' or curtained off: hence 'modesty', 'decency', the qualities of a good official, and so on. He points out that 'metaphor' is Greek for 'transport' and that 'sincere' has Latin roots 'cerus' (cereal) and 'sum' (simple, single), and in Chinese the characters for 'granary' and 'plain', 'simple', are combined to express 'sincere' – the pure grain. Shakespeare has a phrase 'of such a winnowed purity.' Arthur Cooper concludes that the ramifications of this are endless. Unfortunately he died before completing what would have been his seminal book on the subject – *Heart and Mind: Language Making Seen in Early Chinese Script*, although Oxford University Press have commissioned a sinologist to complete the book.

For the modern traveller the railway journey from Beijing to

---

[4]Arthur Cooper, *The Creation of the Chinese Script*, London: The China Society, 1978, p21.

Xi'an via Zhengzhou and Luoyang affords a good view of the loess country: the Great Plain, its endless flatness cut by irrigation channels and long straight roads lined with poplar trees, where the lorries now overtake the traditional carts drawn by teams of three or four horses.

Walled villages, with their accompanying brick kilns, dot the landscape at frequent intervals, and in the dry winter months the entire scene, earth, roads, villages, even the sky, are all one colour, the yellowish-buff of the pervading loess-silt mixture. West of Zhengzhou a dramatic change occurs, as the train threads its way into the loess deposit itself. Fantastic peaks and gullies appear. Here and there are carefully built cultivation terraces sometimes collapsing down the slopes, a reminder of the vulnerability of the loess, not only to erosion, but to the persistent earthquakes which have beset this area from the earliest times, often causing extensive loss of life.

The railway follows the famous old road to the west from Tongguan ('pass') to Luoyang and Xi'an – 'the worst road in the world' according to Richthofen. In the past busy roads gradually sank deep into the soft loess. A traveller in the 1920s reported continual fights between cart drivers whose axles had become locked in narrow stretches of the road.[5] No doubt the first Emperor, Shihuangdi (221 BC), had this problem in mind when he standardized the widths of roads and cart axles to match two thousand years earlier. The same traveller laments: 'In a short time the railway creeping west will join the west and north capitals, and the romance will have vanished.'[6] Romance there may have been, but there was also acute discomfort. Another, commenting on the pre-railway methods of travel, describes the terrible mud of the wet summer and the clouds of dust of the drier seasons.[7] The four-wheeled cart or pack mule was the usual transport, as the sedan chair, used in other parts of China, was not available owing to a lack of bearers. A 'mule

[5]Langdon Warner, *The Long Old Road in China*, London: Arrowsmith, 1927.
[6]W.E. Geil, *The Eighteen Capitals of China*, London: Constable, 1911.
[7]Eric Teichman, *Travels in North West China*, Cambridge: CUP, 1920.

litter' was used by some. This was made of sticks and matting and slung between two mules. 'Not likely to appeal to foreigners as a pleasant method of travel', he comments and goes on to describe the tremendous traffic along the road: carts laden with wheat, cotton and hides hidden in clouds of dust or wallowing in mud according to season. He remarks that travellers going east 'often arrive at Tongguan in a state of collapse.' He recommends a riding pony, and though he admits that this would not suit all travellers, he says that the five-mile amble is less tiring as it is possible to bypass the road by riding through the fields.

From Beijing to Xi'an took 30 days by horse and cart and from Xi'an the famous Old Silk Road started. There were 18 cart stages from Xi'an to Lanzhou, where in the past a bridge of boats crossed the river (Huanghe). Another 20 days brought the traveller to Ganzhou, but this was followed by 18 'bitter stages' to Suzhou (modern Jiuquan) and Hami, then 36 'bitter and sweet' stages to Ürümqi, and 54 more stages to Kashgar. The average distance covered was 30–38km a day, with stopping places every 9–14km. Zhengzhou to Xi'an involved 15 changes and Tongguan to Xi'an took three days. Travellers were catered for by quick meal rooms where sometimes, as noted by a traveller in 1922, the food was quite good. He lists the menu: scrambled eggs, meat balls, chopped pork, chicken, Chinese cabbage with vinegar, griddle cakes, rice and tea[8].

The inns, however, left much to be desired. Langdon Warner describes how he had to place his folding army bed on the kang with each leg in a saucer of oil to keep out the bugs.[9]

What a transformation took place in the next 50 years! In 1976 the three trains from Beijing to Xi'an via Zhengzhou and Luoyang were clean and comfortable. The total travel time was 24 hours. It was November and bitterly cold. The smell of the coke stoves used for warming the trains was reminiscent of old village halls in England. The hotel in Zhengzhou was Russian

---

[8]F.G. Clapp, 'The Hwang ho', *Geographical Review*, 1922, Vol 12, p1.
[9]Langdon Warner, *The Long Old Road in China*, London: Arrowsmith, 1927.

built, mainly to house Soviet advisers. Central heating had been installed, but was not working. The temperature in the bedroom was 12°C but, incredibly, the beds were very warm, thanks to excellent quilts; one had to resist the temptation to cut a small hole to identify the filling! Food and service were very good as on the trains. Giant thermos flasks, often beautifully decorated and filled with near-boiling water, with fine china lidded cups and plentiful tea became a feature of travel which helped greatly against the cold. Seven years later, it came as quite a shock to find that coffee had replaced tea, doubtless a concession to American tourists: a request for tea met with smiling surprise.

The guest house in Luoyang had also been built for Soviet personnel, and the accommodation for two people consisted of a suite of rooms; a flat with two bedrooms, a sitting room furnished with easy chairs, a desk and radio, a bathroom with toilet, and a small extra room which may once have been a kitchen.

In modern times the loess plateau has become one of the poorest regions of China. Problems of drought, flood, and soil erosion have been exacerbated by the spread of cultivation to marginal lands. Recent projects include extensive reafforestation, a 'Green Great Wall' across north China. Changes in farming from crops to animal breeding, for example, rabbits, could be profitable for the small farmer by the sale of meat and skins. No doubt the progress on the 'Taming of the Yellow River' will help to improve water supply, and cut down the huge loss of soil by erosion.

From the earliest beginnings of Chinese civilization the people have wrestled with water problems. Water is the life blood of agriculture: without it the most fertile soil is useless; in the past it could control the success or failure of a community, as is well shown by the history of the great civilizations which flourished by the Nile, the Tigris-Euphrates, and the Indus as well as the Huanghe. During the time of the Warring States (453–221 BC) the prince of Han was anxious to stem the advance of the Qin eastward, so he sent a water engineer, Zheng Guo, to persuade the Qin to build an irrigation canal of more than 300 *li*. This, he hoped, would involve so much labour for a long time, that there would be no chance of further military expansion. Before it was completed, Qin became aware of the trick, and wanted to kill Zheng Guo, who said 'I did deceive you, but this canal would benefit Qin. It will help Han, but sustain Qin for 10,000 generations.' As a result nearly 300,000 hectares were made fertile, with abundant harvests. Qin became rich and powerful, and was able to overcome the other feudal states and found the Chinese Empire in 221 BC.[10]

China has three great river systems: the Changjiang (Yangtze), 6380km long, third in the world after the Amazon and the Nile, the Huanghe (Yellow River), 5464km, and the Xijiang, the river of south China, 2100km. Climatic factors control the flow of water, and for most of the country this means summer rain often causing floods and winter drought calling for irrigation. This is exacerbated by variability in quantity and timing and Chinese history has been punctuated by alternating droughts and floods.

The northern area, particularly the basin of the Huanghe, has the worst problems. Rainfall is light, and occurs mainly as intense storms during the months of June, July and August. Winter is dry and bitterly cold, with the river frozen over for nearly six months. In spring and early summer snow-melt on the mountains and plateaux of Qinghai, the source of the river, produces a surge in the upper reaches, which moves down the river to be amplified later by the summer rains.

After rushing through two gorges, where it is now controlled by the Longyang and Liujia dams, the river slows down in the flatter area surrounding the ancient city of Lanzhou. This was once the site of a bridge of boats, where the Old Silk Road from Xi'an crossed the river. It is now an important industrial centre, depending on electricity generated at the two dams, and is surrounded by irrigated farmland. The dams have reduced the flood flow by as much as 40 per cent.

---

[10]Joseph Needham, *Science and Civilization in China*, Vol 1, Cambridge: CUP, 1954, p285–287.

The river now turns north and then east in what is known as the 'Great Bend'. It was said:

> A hundred harms the Yellow River brings
> But fertile is the soil the Great Bend waters.

Three hundred kilometres from Lanzhou, after another gorge and dam, the river spreads out in braided channels over the flat plain of Ningxia, an Autonomous Region which is home to a Muslim community of seven million people. Hemmed in by a wall of mountains to the west, this area of fertile soil has been cultivated since ancient times. In the past Chinese ingenuity was tested to its limits as the people tried to control the wandering channels, and to water the crops by gravity irrigation. To determine slopes, lines of incense sticks of equal length were carefully 'planted' then lit at night. Simple sluice gates of horizontal and vertical posts which could be moved at will, were used to control and divert the flow. Today the area is covered by a vast web of canals and viaducts, passing under and over each other. In the past as the spring surge moved down the river the rise in water level was monitored and recorded on posts and horsemen galloped ahead to inform watchers down-river of the extent of the oncoming flood.

Navigable waterways have always been extensively used for transport in China. The Huanghe, because of its seasonal variations, and the immense load of silt carried in the lower reaches, has been of only limited use. The Great Bend, from Lanzhou to Baotou, where it turns south to enter the loess area, was navigable for only four months of the year, July to October. It was frozen and shallow from November to March. The thaw came in mid-April, and for a time some ferries and junks were able to operate, but soon the current became too fierce and it was not until July that the river could be fully used. For the next four months, especially for longer journeys, the famous inflated skin rafts of the upper Huanghe came into their own, transporting goods and passengers from Lanzhou to Baotou. The rafts were assembled in western Gansu and floated down to Lanzhou. Most were made from sheep and goat skins, though yaks and bullocks were sometimes used for larger rafts, which could be 9 to 12m long and 3 to 4.5m across, using up to 200 skins. The average size used nine to twelve skins, and would carry six or seven passengers or half a tonne of freight. Single inflated skins were used to assist swimmers.

After killing the animal a small incision was made in a hind leg, and air blown in. It was then pummelled to separate the skin from the flesh. The head was cut off and the hind legs split, and after the hair and wool had been scraped off, the skin was tied at the loins, neck, and forelegs, and a mixture of salt and vegetable oil poured in. The skin was blown orally through a hole in one of the forelegs, being turned from time to time to spread the salt and oil evenly. Finally the skins were lashed to a framework of wooden poles. The raft was propelled by one or more large oars, and during the journey between Lanzhou and Baotou some members of the crew were occupied in mending punctures or repairing damaged skins. Sometimes large rafts consisted of smaller rafts joined together. Large skins, such as those of bullocks or yaks could be used as containers for perishable goods. On reaching Baotou, the rafts were dismantled, the framework sold and the larger undamaged skins were deflated and dried and sent back, formerly by camel caravan, to be sold. Oars were used as shoulder poles by members of the crews to carry back smaller skins. The better parts of damaged skins were made into leather buckets, and the odd pieces into sandals. Not for nothing have the Chinese had the reputation for never wasting anything.

About 200km east of Baotou the river turns south and enters the middle part of its course plunging through the loess plateau. Here one of the main problems of this unruly river appears; the immense load of silt from the erosion of the soft friable loess. There was evidence that this area was once forested, but centuries of drought and human occupation have produced an almost bare landscape vulnerable to the short but intense summer rains. These cause severe gullying and slipping, with resultant landslides. Between 1965 and 1979 more than one thousand occurred, resulting in about two thousand deaths. The Huanghe carries the largest load of sediment of any river in the world, a total of 16,000 million tonnes a year down to the sea. Ninety per cent of this comes from the middle third of its course, where the annual loss of soil is almost incredible; 3,700 tonnes for every square kilometre of land, equivalent to a lowering of the land surface of 25mm per annum. It is estimated that the loss each year is approximately equal to the accumulation of 100 to 300 years which means that the fertile soil is a wasting resource. At times the water becomes so thick with silt that the river resembles a mud flow; 40 per cent by weight above Tongguan in summer. Very rarely it has been known to reach 500 to 700kg per m^3, a more usual figure is 200kg per m^3.

Before debouching on to the Great Plain the Huanghe flows through the San Men ('Three Gates') gorge: the 'Gate of the Gods', 'Gate of the Ghosts', and the 'Gate of Man'. An ancient inscription on a dangerous rock reads 'Come to me: sail in my direction'. By doing so the helmsman could take advantage of a current which avoided the danger.

The great dam at the San Men gorge, built in the earlier stages in the 1950s with Russian help, was intended as the key to the multi-purpose plan to control the Yellow River. The main project involved a 'staircase' of 46 dams of varying size on the upper and middle courses of the river culminating at San Men: in some ways resembling the American plan to 'Walk Big Muddy (the Missouri-Mississippi) down to the sea'. The aim was comprehensive: flood prevention, silt retention, irrigation, hydroelectric power, improvements in navigation, and the control of erosion in the loess.

It is now realized that the scheme was pushed ahead before sufficient basic conservation work had been done. At the same time there was not enough equipment available to cope with the canal construction necessary for irrigation. The severe problem of gullying had not been addressed, in spite of massive do-it-yourself methods by local people. In one area of Shanxi a group of people were said to have been digging every day for 20 years to erect 370 earth and stone dams in 12 large gullies, at the same time building a pumping station, and planting a shelter belt of trees 5km long and 20m wide.

Almost from the beginning in September 1960 accumulation of silt became a major problem at San Men. After only four years, by 1964, water storage in the man-made lake had decreased by 40 per cent owing to deposition. Reconstruction became essential, and today the dam is used as a sediment sluice. Two new by-pass tunnels have been cut in the rock: three of the eight turbine penstocks are used as sluices, and the eight bottom sluices, which were sealed when the dam was completed, have been reopened, to enable the silt-laden flood water to be rushed through as quickly as possible. This has meant a great reduction in generating capacity, from 1200 to 250 megawatts, but the dam still performs a major function in flood control.

Similar methods have proved useful on many of the smaller reservoirs. A hundred kilometres north of Xi'an a reservoir on a tributary of the Yellow River lost 20 per cent of its storage space within three years of its construction and it was estimated that it could only be in use for 10 years.[11] However, by drawing down the water level at the beginning of the flood season, and running the silt-laden water out through sluices, then resuming storage later when the water is cleaner, the possible 'life' of the reservoir has been lengthened to over 80 years. The silty water can be used for irrigation, at the same time fertilizing the soil. Farmers are being encouraged not to cultivate steep fields, to substitute pasture for ploughing as erosion is less where grass binds the soil, to plant trees, plug the gullies, and build terraces as in the past, but only where they can be reasonably maintained. The old saying in north China 'When the river runs clear,' meaning 'Never', will hopefully become outdated in time as will the epithet 'China's Sorrow' for the Huanghe.

The Great Plain of north China owes its existence to the Yellow River, which over many thousands of years deposited

---

[11] *Geographical Magazine*, June 1981.

millions of tonnes of sediment, extending its delta into what was once a gulf of the sea. The Gulf of Bohai and the Yellow Sea were joined west of the present Shandong peninsula, then a group of islands. The sands and silts of the Great Plain are almost 1000m thick, accumulating in a sinking area of the earth's crust.

As the Plain extended, the river meandered slowly across the flat expanse, silting up its channel until the bed and banks were raised above the general ground level so that to a distant viewer it appeared like a range of low hills. A surge or slight change of current could easily lead to a breach of the bank, causing the entire river to overflow and change course. During the past 3000 years there have been 1500 such breaches and 26 changes of course, 9 of them very extensive: 15 different channels were used by the river (i.e. some used more than once).

Until 602 BC it is known that the Huanghe flowed out north east to the Gulf of Bohai, not very far from its present position. It then swung south of the Shandong peninsula across the plain and out into the Yellow Sea for nearly 700 years, when it turned north east once more. In 1324 it swung south again for 500 years and in 1851 another great change brought it back to the Gulf of Bohai. In 1938 the Guomindang (Nationalist Government under Chiang Kai-Shek), in an effort to stem the Japanese invasion, cut the dykes at Huayuankou, north east of Zhengzhou, causing a huge flood. The Huanghe became part of the Huai river. Twelve million people were affected and about 900,000 died.

At the end of World War II, from December 1946 to May 1947, with the help of UNRRA[12], the river was forced back to a north east direction. An earth dyke and a rock filled dam, using 30,600m^3 of rock were built. Kaoliang stalks, millet straw and willow branches were brought by ox cart, and hemp (for rope) by train. Two and a half million jute bags were imported from India and 240,000 board metres of timber from

[12]United Nations Relief and Rehabilitation Administration.

Oregon USA. 40,000 Chinese farmers using their own simple tools cut four channels 3 to 16km long, 18m wide and 1.5 to 2m deep.

In the years since 1949, more than 2000km of dykes have been built along the river and 5000 mattress revetments replaced by stone-faced walls, curved to impede the force of the flow. This method is now often applied to sea defences in Britain and elsewhere. The flat surfaces presented by walls in the past often proved inadequate in resisting wave attack.

In 1958 a big rise in the level of the Huanghe came within half a metre of the top of the new dykes. More than a million workers were called up to add 1m to the dykes along a 600km stretch, and they held. There has been no serious breach since 1949. In the absence of bed-rock, the stone facing can collapse, so constant inspection is vital, and stockpiles of stones must be maintained for emergencies. On the landward side, where the dykes tend to be unstable, land level is now raised by siphoning off silt-laden water and using the settlement basins for crops.

The area near Zhengzhou, where the main dyke had been cut in 1938, became alkaline and sandy. A pool was created behind the dyke and filled with silt to form fresh farmland, which became the prosperous commune of Huayuankou. A visit to Zhengzhou, now an important industrial city and railway junction, can give some idea of the immense labour involved in the effort to control the Yellow River. There is an attractive museum in the city, the 'Museum of the Taming of the Yellow River' with excellent models and illuminated maps. In 1976 an added bonus for visitors was a delightful reception room decked out in green and gold, with matching chairs and curtains and a row of elegant gilded thermos flasks of hot water. An interesting and informative lecture on the problem of the Huanghe was delivered, while the visitors sipped quantities of jasmine tea from green and gold lidded cups.

Between Zhengzhou and the sea, there were now 560 pumping stations large and small. A good example of an important one is at Mangshan, 45km from Zhengzhou. It was completed in two years, from 1970 to 1972, mainly by a force of 70,000 volunteers who donated a total of four million working days. It was financed from local resources with no contribution from the state. Water is pumped up the hillside in two stages (33 and 53m) to irrigate 19,000*mu* (over 1200ha) of terraced fields. Five tunnels take water to the city and a hydro-electric station generates local power.

The view from above the power station gives a vivid impression, both of the loess and of the great river. In parts the loess landscape has a desert-like appearance, though lacking the smooth surfaces of sand dunes. Nearer the pumping station neatly cut terraces are planted with hundreds of trees to hold the loose earth. The river (in November) stretches away to the horizon, a flat yellow expanse of sand, intersected by several major streams and many small meandering ones. Two bridges, rail and road, appear to converge across the river, fading into a yellow haze concealing the far bank. They appear abnormally low in the water, emphasising the shallowness of the Huanghe even when in spate, but as those familiar with British coasts will know, rushing shallow water can be dangerous. The Huanghe at full flow must be a menacing sight. An early traveller on the old Beijing-Guangzhou railway wrote of the sensation of intense shaking felt in the train as the bridge vibrated violently in the middle section of the turbulent river.

For centuries on the Great Plain the only solution to flooding has been to raise the dykes ever higher, leaving sufficient space between them to allow the river plenty of room. Often a width of 8 to 12km was left, but as the flow in Zhengzhou can vary from 800m^3 per second in winter to as much as 20,000 in summer this was not always sufficient. Aerial photographs of the Plain reveal myriads of faint lines marking the position of ancient dykes.

The future control of this unruly river depends not only on the maintenance of the modern dykes, but also on measures to reduce the amount of silt carried. The delta is still growing out into the Bohai Gulf at the rate of 10km per annum seaward along a 60km front. In the delta area it is said that it is impossible to identify land and sea. Fishermen on stilts gather their catch in a sea of liquid yellow mud.

2

CHINESE CITIES: XI'AN, ANCIENT AND MODERN

It is interesting that the Chinese word for 'wall' is also used for 'city'. By 1400 BC Anyang, the capital of the Shang dynasty, was already a considerable city, as indeed its predecessor near present-day Zhengzhou, had been. In common with ancient cities elsewhere, there was always a cosmic element to the Chinese city; the symbolism developed from the concept of man's place in the universe and what has been called the Qi or 'breath, the life movement of the spirit through the rhythm of things.' The siting of a city, or a ruler's palace, must be in harmony with this, finding a balance between the Yang and Yin, the male and female 'currents' to the east and west of the site and between hill and valley, using the protection of winding rivers and sheltering hills, avoiding the 'danger' of bare rocks, or open spaces where the 'breath' would be scattered. All this amounts to conforming with the *feng-shui*, the spirits of wind and water. The main north-south axis of a city should be aligned with the Pole Star and the shadow of the noon-day sun. In the *Book of Songs* we read:

> The Ting star is in the middle of the sky;
> We begin to build the palace at Ch'u.
> Orienting them by the rays of the Sun
> We set to work on the houses at Ch'u.[13]

---

[13] *Book of Songs*, trans. Arthur Waley, London: George Allen and Unwin, 1969, p281, No 256.

Geomancers and astrologers were employed in the choice of sites for cities and important buildings as indeed they still are in present day Hong Kong, where the most modern business men and bankers are only too pleased to adhere to their advice in order to keep the all important work force happy. 'We must go along with the staff's beliefs.' In Kowloon (meaning 'nine dragons') the nine dragons who were said to pass through the lobby of the Regent Hotel each morning for a bathe in the harbour were frustrated by the building. However the *feng-shui* man said they were able to pass through glass, so a glass wall was specially built for them. It was 80m long and 12m high – result: booming business! The Connaught Centre has hundreds of round windows which meant that bad spirits could get in, but not out. The *feng-shui* man advised replacement with reflective glass, in which they would see their own image and be frightened away. This was done.

The essentials of an ancient city were the walls of pounded earth, which were built first, followed by the ramparts, moats and gates, the Altar of Earth and Soil, and the ancestral shrine of the local lord or duke. These sacred shrines were situated to the east and west of the main north-south street which ran from the 'palace' in the centre to the south gate. Traditionally there were twelve gates representing the twelve months of the year. The public market was usually to the north of the town, as commercial activity was regarded as profane. Artisans and merchants lived near the market, farmers near the gates, and the poor and destitute near or even within the walls. Outside the walls, and later enclosed by additional walls, were handicraft workshops, centres of commercial activity and industries, as well as residential suburbs, and burial grounds, and beyond this the farmland on which the city depended for food. Many of the inhabitants spent the winter in the city and the summer in the countryside. In time an urban aristocracy developed, serviced by peasant serfs who paid their taxes in grain. This was stored in the city centre and supported the hosts of conscripts required not only for the army, but also for water conservation, flood control, and the maintenance of canals and irrigation systems.

In the Neolithic village of Banpo a foretaste of some of these features can be identified. No doubt there was a Holy Place somewhere in the centre where the local lord performed the rites to ensure a good harvest. Many ancient sites have revealed an area of tamped earth raised above the general level.

Gradually a hierarchy of towns and cities evolved. In the ancient *Book of Yin* we find the following: 'Any metropolitan city whose wall is more than 3000 cubits (5.5km) round is a danger to the state. According to the regulations of the former kings such a city of the first order can have its wall only one-third as long as that of the capital, one of the second order only one-fifth as long, and one of the least order only one-ninth.'[14] The typical small walled cities grew in number from the 11th to the 6th centuries BC and by Han times (200 BC) were spread over North China. The basic plan, laid down in ancient times, persisted there for over 2000 years. The rectangular area was divided into four walled quarters to correspond with the four seasons, and the houses, averaging 100 to a quarter, each stood in a walled enclosure. The householder going out of the city passed through three gates, that of the house, the quarter, and the city. All were shut and locked at night and at one time the penalty for trespass was the loss of a foot. This arrangement was strictly adhered to from Qin times (221 to 207 BC). It not only facilitated social control such as the call-up of conscripts for the army or communal labour: but also the taking of the census, which at one time occurred in the 8th month of each year.

As time passed new towns with no political function were founded and in Central and South China commercial cities assumed many different shapes, though the inner city areas remained rectangular. A Portuguese traveller visiting

[14] *Annals of the Association of American Geographers*, 1952, Vol XIII: quoted from the *Chinese Classics: Book of Songs,* trans. J. Legge, Hong Kong, 1871, Vol 5, Part 1, p5. A cubit was probably 8 Chinese feet.

Guangzhou in the 16th century described 'very fine suburbs where streets were locked at night and guarded.'[15]

Imperial capitals, being larger than other cities, did not always conform exactly to the traditional layout. The great Tang city of Chang'an was an example of this. In 581 AD when Emperor Wen of the Sui dynasty decided to build a splendid new capital, the site had already been in use for 2000 years. The capital of the Western Zhou was established here after the conquest of Shang in 1027 BC, and ended in 771 BC with the move to Luoyang, where it remained for the next 500 years. In 221 BC the Qin emperor Shihuangdi built his capital Xianyang 20km north-west of present Xi'an. At one time, obsessed by the fear of assassination, he built a series of palaces on the outskirts and moved constantly from one to another, so that his whereabouts was always uncertain. The succeeding Han dynasty continued with their capital Chang'an until the movement to Luoyang in 220 AD, thus repeating the experience of the Zhou.

Life at Court and in the capital for the scholar gentry, and indeed for the rich merchants had reached a peak of luxury during the Han dynasty, particularly after the capital moved to Luoyang. Regulations which prevented merchants and artisans from using horses and carriages, or wearing silk or jade, were not always enforced as the officials relied on the traders and craftsmen for many of their luxuries. Increasing trade along the Silk Road, and by sea via Guangzhou brought carpets and jewellery, ornaments and spices, from India, SE Asia and the Middle East, while from western Central Asia (after the defeat of Ferghana in 102 BC) came thousands of the famous 'blood-sweating horses whose stock is the offspring of supernatural horses'. The Han emperor Wudi had sent an emissary to Yue Chi to ask for help against the Xiongnu (Huns) who had overrun the western regions, but his request was refused and Zhang Qian (the emissary) was imprisoned for 10 years. He

---

[15]Gaspar da Cruz, *South China in the 16th Century*, London: Hakluyt Society, 1953.

escaped to Ferghana, and reported the existence of these very fine horses. The emperor sent a gold statuette of a horse, with an offer to purchase, but the people of Ferghana refused. The envoys broke up the statuette and fled, but were killed on the frontier. The emperor then dispatched an army of 60,000, who defeated Ferghana in 102 BC, and brought back some of the excellent horses and more than 3000 stallions and mares of lesser breeds.

By 581 AD the site of Han Chang'an was in ruins, and regarded as haunted, although the surrounding area was fertile and well populated. However, a new site nearby was approved by the geomancers. Their axial line turned out to be only 16 minutes west of true north.

The first Sui city which arose on this site later became the capital of the great Tang dynasty, often regarded as China's 'Golden Age'. At its peak Tang Chang'an was the largest city in the world, with a population of about two million if 'suburbs' outside the walls are included. It differs from the basic city plan in several ways. The Palace area was against the North wall instead of in the centre. This resulted in there being nine gates, three on each of the East, West and South walls, instead of the usual twelve. The Altar of Earth and the Royal Ancestral Temple were in the usual position, and the administrative buildings were south of the Palace. The market area was in two parts. The upper classes lived in the eastern part of the city, and their market was less busy and gradually became more of a residential area. The western market on the other hand, was intensely busy and crowded with people of all types: not only merchants and traders, always regarded as second-class citizens by the Chinese élite, but street performers such as acrobats, jugglers, actors and story-tellers. Traders from distant regions along the famous Silk Road were often seen there: Turks, Syrians, Tartars and Tibetans as well as Buddhist monks from faraway India.

Twenty-five broad carriage roads crossed the city, 14 from east to west, and 11 from north to south, the latter being more than 120m wide and the east-west ones a little less. They were lined with ditches and footpaths and planted with fruit trees.

At night all gates were closed and silence reigned but for the sound of the official patrols of horsemen riding up and down the streets.

The famous Tang poet Bai Juyi (772–846) described a night view of the city:

> Hundreds of houses, thousands of houses – like a great chess board.
> The twelve streets like a huge field planted with rows of cabbage.
> In the distance I see faint and small the torches of riders to Court,
> Like a single row of stars lying to the west of the Five Gates.[16]

As in all Chinese cities, there were areas used for cultivation, private gardens and imperial and private parks. There was an Imperial Park near the Palace north of the city wall, and in the south-east the famous Zhu Jiang water park, used mainly by the upper classes. We are told that Bai Juyi 'liked to go there on horseback, dismount and stroll among the willows along its bank. Richly planted with trees and flowers, including willows, poplars, pink lotuses, marsh grasses and reeds, and attracting wildfowl of every sort, the gardens brought visitors from among the élite every season.'[17]

Life at the court was vividly described by poets of the time, particularly two of the greatest Tang poets Du Fu (712–770) and Bai Juyi (772–846). Poets were members of the educated élite, and often held official positions. They frequently expressed social and political opinions in poems and ballads, the equivalent of the European pamphleteers of a much later date. Tang poetry was normally set to music, and a popular song could reach a very large number of people. Here are three

---

[16]Arthur Waley, *Chinese Poems*, London: George Allen and Unwin, 1961, p161.

[17]Yi-Fu Tuan: *China*, (Vol 1 of The World's Landscapes), Harlow: Longmans, 1970, p108.

examples. The first is taken from the *Ballad of the Beautiful Ladies* by Du Fu:

Spring festival and spring
Is truly in the air: by the winding stream at Chang'an
Lovely ladies walk, looking
Proudly ahead, then exchanging
Sweet and charming smiles with
Each other: faces so beautiful
Perfect figures showing through silk
Draperies embroidered with
Golden peacocks or silver unicorns:
Their heads dressed in kingfisher
Colours with hanging pendants of
Cut jade: on their backs little
Overgarments studded with pearls
Amongst this galaxy the sisters
Of Yang Kuei Fei, bearing great titles.
Dishes served the purple meat
Of camel's hump with slices of raw
Fish on crystal plates; yet these
Hardly satisfy jaded taste: all that
Has taken so much thought and work
To prepare, left hardly touched.
Palace servants ride carefully, bring
New dishes from the Imperial kitchens:
The orchestra gives such music that
Even the hearts of devils are moved:
Important guests and their retinues
Crowd in: at last comes the Greatest
Nonchalantly on his horse: alights
In the most important spot: catkins
Have fallen so thickly as to have
Covered spring grasses, and
With sure steps he strides across them;
Overhead, a bluebird flies off with
A red kerchief it has picked up;
Prime Minister Yang is all-powerful

His slightest touch will burn;
Best to keep clear of him and his
Evil temper.[18]

The second is from *The Flower Market* by Bai Juyi:

In the Royal City spring is almost over;
Tinkle, tinkle – the coaches and horsemen pass.
We tell each other 'This is the peony season';
And follow with the crowd that goes to the Flower Market.
'Cheap and dear – no uniform price;
The cost of the plant depends on the number of blossoms.
For the fine flower a hundred pieces of damask;
For the cheap, five bits of silk.
Above is spread an awning to protect them;
Around is woven a wattle-fence to screen them.
If you sprinkle water and cover the roots with mud,
When they are transplanted, they will not lose their beauty.'
Each household thoughtlessly follows the custom,
Man by man, no one realizing.
There happened to be an old farm labourer
  Who came by chance that way.
He bowed his head and sighed a deep sigh;
But this sigh nobody understood.
He was thinking, 'A cluster of deep-red flowers
Would pay the taxes of ten poor houses.'[19]

And the last from the collection *Song and Dance* by Bai Juyi – the 9th of the 10 *Songs of Qin*:

In Ch'ang-an the year draws to its close;
A great snow fills the Royal Domain.

---

[18]Arthur Waley, *Translations from the Chinese*, London: Visual Publications, 1973.
[19]Arthur Waley, *Chinese Poems*, London: George Allen and Unwin, 1961, p121.

And through the storm, on their way back from Court,
In reds and purples the dukes and barons ride.
They can enjoy the beauty of wind and snow;
To the rich they do not mean hunger and cold.
At a grand entry coaches and riders press;
Candles are lit in the Tower of Dance and Song.
Delighted guests pack knee to knee;
Heated with wine they throw off their double furs.
The host is high in the Board of Punishments;
The chief guest comes from the Ministry of Justice.
It was broad daylight when the drinking and music began;
Midnight has come, and still the feast goes on.
What do they care at Wên-hsiang to-night
In the town gaol prisoners are freezing to death?[20]

To anyone interested in Chinese history a visit to Xi'an is a delight. The past permeates the atmosphere and reverberates from beneath one's feet. 'The great joy of the town was to be in it,' wrote an enthusiastic traveller in the 1920s.[21] The modern city of Xi'an only partly covers the site of the splendid Tang capital, which was about seven times as large. After the fall of the dynasty in 907 AD, decline set in, and during the next 500 years it was never to regain its former glory. Kaifeng and Hangzhou served as capitals during the Song dynasty, Beijing (then called Cambaluc) at the time of Kublai Khan and the visit of Marco Polo, to be followed by Nanjing in the early Ming dynasty. The final move to Beijing was made by the Ming emperor Yongle in the early 15th century. At the same time a sort of last gesture was made to Chang'an when a palace was built there for the Emperor's son, and the present-day walls of the city were built. However the lapse into semi-isolation continued until modern communications were

[20]Arthur Waley, *Life and Times of Po Chü-i*, London: George Allen and Unwin, 1970, p63.
[21]Langdon Warner, *The Long Old Road in China*, London: Arrowsmith, 1927, Chap 1.

developed, and Xi'an became one of Communist China's designated inland industrial centres.

In November 1976 when the writer was there a spirit of euphoria was abroad after the elimination of the 'Gang of Four' and the end of the tyrannies of the Cultural Revolution. A group of British tourists, one of whom was an architect and town-planner who made the request, were fortunate to be granted an evening session with some of Xi'an's city planners who came to the Renmin Hotel to talk about the future of their city. It was a freezing evening, and there was no heating. The planners did not discard their padded outdoor clothing, and the tourists were advised to collect blankets from their beds. Thus cocooned and warmed by the enthusiasm of the city planners they shared their dreams for a new and splendid Xi'an to be equal in size to the great Tang city of a thousand years ago.

On the northern side the railway and the Wei river were to remain the boundary, whilst development was envisaged to the east, west and south. Main roads averaging in width 15–20m were to be widened where possible to 30–40m with bicycle lanes separated from other traffic by lines of trees. Industrial areas would be created to the east and west while the south would be reserved for cultural and educational developments. Pollutant industries would be sited on the urban borders, with recycling facilities incorporated into new factories, and the resultant purified liquids used for irrigation. Industrial housing would be built near factories to minimise the journey to work. Each neighbourhood would contain primary schools, clinics, bookshops, post offices and banks as well as food shops and service centres for repairs and laundry. All would be within cycling distance of people's homes, to reduce the burden on the local authorities. Hospitals and middle schools, and small factories for clothing and processed foods would be more widely distributed. With the Chinese love of statistics they quoted developments which had taken place between 1949 and 1976: more than 20 million m^2 of building, 4 million m^2 of roads and paving surfaces of asphalt and cement, four major waterworks, three public gardens and over 400 buses and trolley buses brought into use.

Attention has been directed to the preservation of ancient monuments and the provision of museums such as that at Banpo. The area around Xi'an teems with archaeological treasures to an extent that it is difficult to match the building of museums with the pace of new discoveries. In spite of some vandalism by the 'Red Guards' the ten years of the Cultural Revolution (1966–1976) had seen a boom in archaeology culminating in 1974 in the sensational discovery of the 'terracotta warriors' of the first Emperor's tomb.

In 1976 houses and flats built by the municipality of Xi'an were all for rent, which was minimal and for maintenance only. It included winter heating, a life-saving necessity in the short but bitter winters of North China. In rural areas peasants could build and own their houses, which could not be sold, but handed down to family members only. Factories often provided cheap accommodation for young people in dormitories, or with two sharing a room. The general impression on a Western visitor was of a standard of living below that of Western Europe, but of a society simply but adequately fed and clothed, with rising standards of education and medical care. Children looked healthy and lively and were often dressed in bright colours not yet available for adults, who were still in their 'Mao suits', a blue-grey uniform, but well padded against the winter wind. People appeared hard-working, purposeful and cheerful, with a great capacity for enjoyment of music, acrobatic and juggling performances, and the traditional Chinese opera and theatre, now emerging from the strait-jacket of the Cultural Revolution.

1976 had been a year of tremendous events in China, with the deaths of Zhou Enlai and Mao Zedong, the downfall of the 'Gang of Four', and in July, the terrible Tangshan earthquake. Among the peasants this last event must have reinforced the ancient belief in the link between momentous events in Nature and in the world of men. Aftershocks of the great quake had been experienced in Beijing for some time, one of which shook down part of the façade of the Russian-built Beijing Hotel. Xi'an is known to be on a direct earthquake line from Beijing, and the city had been warned to expect at least aftershocks, if not a major quake. The outcome was that the pavements of all the main streets were blocked by temporary earthquake shelters, built for flat-dwellers to use at night for sleeping. All kinds of materials had been utilized from straw, cloth, and wood to the pavement trees which served as support posts. Fortunately most road traffic then consisted of bicycles, otherwise the total loss of pavements could have been a hazard. The effect of an almost continuous line of make-shift housing, often with trees sprouting through the roofs was odd indeed, and made shopping quite difficult.

In 1989 when the writer again visited Xi'an many changes had taken place. The rather bleak Russian-built Renmin Hotel had been replaced by a smart new 559 room building in the modern international style, complete with shopping centre, swimming pool, 14 dining rooms offering Chinese and Western food, bars, and a gymnasium: also all facilities for business men and such extra services as film developing and printing, massage, and bicycle hire. Many small streets had been paved, traffic lights installed, and sports grounds, department stores and a large covered market constructed. In side streets and every nook and alley in main roads, small 'private enterprise' efforts proliferated, with food shops cooking meals while you wait and small stalls with everything from drinks and fruit to shoes and sandals, clothes, bicycle repairs and instant silhouette 'portraits'. Industries had been developed such as textiles, chemicals and electrical components, the new factories often with adjoining high-rise flats for the workers. Ancient crafts continued to flourish, and the Arts and Handicrafts factory which was a centre of excellence in 1976 making exquisite lacquer screens for export as well as carvings in ivory and shell and elaborate feather pictures, was busier than ever in 1989. A whole new section had been added to cope with the immense demand for models in all sizes of the 'terracotta warriors'.

The opening up of the tomb of the first Emperor Qin Shihuangdi (221–210 BC) had barely begun in 1976, which was only two years after some peasants digging a well had suddenly come upon the life-size figures of warriors of 2000 years ago. Thus began one of the greatest archaeological dramas of the

20th century. Although tradition had described the splendours of the tomb itself, no one suspected the existence of a guardian underground army. Here were 6000 soldiers in battle array, complete with chariots and horses, and details of armour and uniforms from the insignia of rank down to belt buckles and the soles of boots. Weapons included swords, spears and halberds, and the deadly crossbow invented in China in the 5th century BC, which was a vital factor in securing the victories of the Qin and the foundation of the empire. Many of the weapons are still sharp after 2000 years owing to the incorporation of a chromium coating on the bronze.

The terracotta figures of men and horses were expertly modelled in local clay, fired at high temperatures and then painted. Enough traces of paint survive to give some idea of the splendour of the original scene. A huge structure resembling an aeroplane hangar has been built over the site and a raised walkway surrounds the excavated area, which is about 1.5km east of the tomb. Years of work lie ahead before the archaeologists reach the tomb itself. The present director has said that it will be his grandson who will experience that great moment. With their innate feeling for history the Chinese can be relied upon not to indulge in any unseemly haste. The uncovering of such a vast treasure house calls for immense patience and skill. The tomb is said to have contained a marble map of the Chinese Empire with rivers of mercury, roofed with a dome showing the constellations, not to mention the treasures of the actual sarcophagus of the Emperor. No one knows however, whether tomb robbers ever found it: we can only wait. Early in 1992 it was announced that an excavation at the tomb mound itself had been suspended. Several reasons were given: first, the actual tomb is covered by 100m of earth; the removal of this constitutes a formidable challenge. Secondly the water table is 16m from the surface: this means extensive pumping will need to be installed: time is needed to work out the implications of this. Thirdly, a huge hangar, at least 500m square will need to be built over the tomb.

For the modern visitor, the present display of 1000 of the 6000 warriors is impressive enough. Passing through the normal Western-type museum entrance one is suddenly confronted by Shihuangdi's 'spirit army'. There they stand facing east, ready to repulse any attack on the tomb from spirit armies from that quarter seeking revenge for the defeats inflicted by the emperor during his lifetime. In the vanguard three rows of bowmen prepare to launch the blizzard of arrows and murderous cross-bow bolts which preceded the main attack, in much the same way as the artillery barrage cleared the way for the trench battles of World War I. These warriors wear no armour nor helmets, probably to facilitate speed of movement. Their varied and complicated hairstyles may be an indication of rank or function. Behind them, in eleven corridors originally paved with brick and roofed with timber, fibre matting, and plaster, stands the main body of armoured infantry, accompanied by six four-horse wooden chariots driven by officers. An astonishing feature of this army is that unlike the miniatures often found in tombs these soldiers are slightly larger than life and their facial features have been individually modelled; no two are alike: were they copied from real people? All the variety of Chinese types is there: mainly men from the north-west, the present day provinces of Shaanxi and Gansu, but also some minority nationalities and men from Shu (modern Sichuan). Expressions vary from stern to thoughtful, serene and dignified to nervous. The effect on the viewer is quite different from that of an ordinary museum visit. These are not just pottery models: they are works of art, a sculptured portrait gallery of ancient China. One has to remember that at the time of Shihuangdi Chinese civilization was already well over 1000 years old.

No doubt much hidden treasure remains to be unearthed at this unique site. In 1976 a second pit was excavated. It contained over 300 crossbowmen, chariots and cavalry. A third smaller pit seems to have contained a command post. In 1980 an excavation to the west of the tomb mound revealed two bronze chariots each with charioteers and four horses about two-thirds life size. The workmanship is exquisite and each chariot has 3000 components.

These discoveries have put Xi'an on the tourist map in a big way. Even the shortest package tours now include a visit to the terracotta warriors. About 24km east of the city the coaches debouch at another tourist 'hot spot', the famous Huaqing Springs. These were discovered in Western Zhou times (1027–771 BC) when a palace was built there. The first emperor added a concubine's bath, and succeeding dynasties contributed various buildings. The site became a favourite venue for outings by the rich of Xi'an.

In 1976, 24 of us had the place almost to ourselves. Some bathed in the warm spring water, others climbed the steep mountain path for the stupendous view over the rich farmland of the Wei valley and saw far off, the mound of Shihuangdi's tomb. En route we were shown the site of the 'Xi'an incident' of 1936, when Chiang Kai-Shek was captured by the Communists. The guide was delighted to point out the window ledge where he had left his false teeth as he attempted to escape. He was of course recaptured and forced to sign an agreement for a joint effort against the Japanese.

By 1989 the place had been transformed. It was almost standing room only. The steps down to the lake were solid with people. Such was the press that it was difficult to take a walk in any direction, but the little lake shimmered in the April sunshine, surrounded by beautiful trees, the translucent green of the spring willows falling to the water's edge, while the red pillars and golden roofs of the buildings soared into the blue sky above the crowds. Even the new densely packed coach park could not mar the enchantment of the place.

Xi'an now has a population of two million, equal to that of Tang Chang'an, and is the capital of Shaanxi. The Provincial Museum, housed in a former Confucian temple is one of the best in China, with sections on archaeology and history arranged in order of dynasties, and about 70 stone sculptures of animals, including one of a rhinoceros. The most interesting section 'the best thing in town' according to Langdon Warner[22] is the Beilin, or 'Forest of Stone Tablets', a collection

[22]Langdon Warner, *The Long Old Road in China*, London: Arrowsmith, 1927, Chap 1.

of over a thousand inscribed tablets, each about 2 by 0.75m mounted on a stone tortoise, the symbol of longevity, and showing not only the evolution of Chinese calligraphy, but also the teachings of Confucius, written on 13 tablets. These were commissioned by a Tang emperor who was anxious to preserve for future generations the authentic words of the sage. Some tablets have poems and sometimes illustrations of trees, flowers and bamboo. Rubbings of these are sold in great numbers to visiting tourists.

One famous stone needs special mention, the so-called 'Nestorian Stone' dated 781 AD. It was discovered by Jesuits outside the west gate of the city in 1625, and caused astonishment as it shows a Christian cross cut in the stone and records in Chinese and Syriac the story of Nestorian Christianity in the Tang capital from 631 AD. The religion had come to China along the Old Silk Road from Persia, and in 638 AD permission was obtained to preach and to build churches, but in 842 the banning of all foreign religions took place, and Nestorianism vanished from China, never to return except for a short-lived revival during the Yuan (Mongol) dynasty. Buddhism suffered greatly at this time as Daoist and Confucian ideas reasserted themselves.

Another point of interest for the visitor is the Big Wild Goose (or Great Gander) Pagoda. On the south side of the city today, it was well within the boundary of Tang Chang'an. The pagoda was built to store the Buddhist documents brought back from India by the monk Xuan Zang in 645 AD. He had set off in 629 to study Buddhism in the land of its origin, and to try to resolve some of the contradictions existing among the Buddhist philosophers of the time. After two years in Kashmir and a visit to Bodh Gaya, the site of Buddha's Enlightenment, he lived for seven years at the great monastery of Nalanda in Northern India. He was treated as an honoured guest, allotted ten lay servants, instead of the usual two. The monastery was home to 11,000 monks, and owned large tracts of fertile land with more than 100 villages, which supplied daily deliveries of food. The peaceful security of their lives enabled the monks to concentrate on their mental and spiritual development to the extent that they came to regard the material world as an illusion.

Xuan Zang became a master of Sanskrit, and on his return to China organized a team of translators who worked with him until the end of his life in 664. During this time they achieved a quarter of all the Sanskrit-Chinese translations made during a period of 600 years. The procedures he adopted have been cited as a foretaste of methods used by modern lexicographers and linguistic experts. 1,300 volumes were produced by his Board of Translators. Xuan Zang himself worked to a very strict schedule, sleeping only from 10pm until 2am, when he read through the next day's work, marking words in order in red. Twice a day he lectured to monk-students – there were over 100 in the monastery. He also received orders for translation from the Palace, such as a request from the king of Assam for a copy of the *Daodejing* in Sanskrit.

The Tang emperor Tai Zong was a great admirer of Xuan Zang. He came out in person to welcome the monk when he returned from India, and gave him every facility for his work. At one time he presented him with a cassock 'worth 100 pieces of gold and so finely stitched that one could not see where the threads came in and out.' Tai Zong died in 649 AD.

Great processions were held to celebrate great occasions, such as the return of Xuan Zang from India, when the holy objects he had brought back were displayed to the public: images of the Buddha in gold, silver and sandalwood, 657 books and a casket containing 150 pellets of Buddha's flesh. Another occasion was at the end of 648 when the images and books were carried from one monastery to another. We are told that the 'Nine Palace Orchestras' played mainly foreign music, an indication of the cosmopolitan nature of Chang'an. On the gate tower of the Palace were assembled the Emperor, the Crown Prince and the Court ladies, all swinging incense burners. In the procession were monks, politicians, generals, soldiers, mummers, a stage lion, musicians and dancers who performed a song-dance entitled *The Breaking of the Ranks*, commemorating the victory of the Emperor Tai Zong, when still a prince, over the last opponents of the Tang dynasty in

620. This dance became a sort of Chinese dance-anthem and was performed at important weddings and other occasions.[23]

Xuan Zang suggested to the new emperor that a pagoda should be erected to store the scriptures and images brought from India, and the volumes of translations. He wanted it built of stone, and about 100m high. The emperor demurred because of the expense, and suggested brick and a height of 40m. The money was raised by the sale of missing people's clothing, which seems to have been a normal method of fund raising. The pagoda was completed in 652, and in that year an Indian monk from Bodh Gaya arrived, bringing a letter for Xuan Zang, and a present. 'We send you herewith a pair of white cotton sheets to show that we have not forgotten you.'

Not far from the Big Wild Goose Pagoda is the Small Wild Goose Pagoda, its top still bearing the scar of the 16th century earthquake. In common with other typical Chinese cities, Xi'an still has a Drum Tower and a Bell Tower. The latter is at an important central cross road, and in 1976 the 15th century bell was still rung at dawn. Alas, it has now been replaced by a lamp.

On the outskirts of modern Xi'an the high-rise blocks are sprouting, but a short distance along the road to Huaqing suddenly there is a wall painted with chariots and horses galloping towards the city. 'The boundary of a Tang hunting park' says the guide in a flat voice. In the Western half of the city is the great mosque, a series of courtyards packed with buildings, their curved roofs soaring gracefully upwards, apparently typically Chinese. An old man shuffles along the path, his long robe and skull cap, his short white beard, and slightly aquiline nose in an essentially Chinese face, reminiscent of the days when Xi'an was a melting pot of peoples. At the time of its greatest splendour, Chang'an must have been the most cosmopolitan city in the world. The echoes of the past reverberate down the ages: after all, what is a thousand years

---

[23]Arthur Waley, *The Real Tripitaka*, London: George Allen and Unwin, 1952, p26–28.

but ‘an evening gone’ in the history of man? ‘The great joy of the town was to be in it’ is as true in the nineties as it was 70 years ago.

3

DOWN THE LONG RIVER (I)
The 'Paradise on Earth'

The second great river of China, the Yangtze, known in the main part of its course as the Changjiang (Long River) is the third longest river in the world. Its actual source has been confirmed only recently in a survey completed in 1979. The population of its basin totals something like 300 million, three times that of the Huanghe.

Both rivers begin on the high plateau of Tibet, the Huanghe soon establishing a north-easterly course, while the Changjiang plunges south, a raging torrent running parallel to the great ranges east of the Himalayas whose deep and sometimes inaccessible valleys with their pools of stagnant air, also carry the two great rivers of South-East Asia, the Salween and the Mekong. Geologists tell us that this whole area of the earth's crust is still rising gently, thus enhancing the cutting of the ever deepening valleys. At a point within 100km of the Burmese frontier the three great rivers almost converge, but while the Salween and the Mekong continue south, the Changjiang zigzags away to the east, cutting across several ranges to emerge at the river port of Yibin, in the south-west corner of the province of Sichuan.

Throughout this mountainous part of its course, the Changjiang is known by a different name, the Jinshajiang, or 'River of Golden Sands'. For centuries the local people have been panning for gold along its banks. Today there is a modern panning machine at Baiyu,[24] worked by Han Chinese as the

[24]*China Reconstructs*, June 1988, p68.

Tibetans lack the necessary skills. Local people pan among the dregs left by the machine and one family was recorded as having raised itself from poverty to the 'middle income' group in two years. Recently Philip Short, BBC correspondent in Beijing, travelled to the Jinshajiang beyond Yibin, and found that peasants were spending about three months each year, in the dry season, panning for gold, and achieving an average of 3.5oz per annum which they sell to the Government for £500 equivalent and 1.5 tons of rice as a welcome addition to their incomes. He also commented that many features of 'Old China' can still be seen beyond Yibin: for example, 'trackers' hauling junks up the river, which lacks any navigation aids. At the point where navigation ends a large rock once bore an inscription 'The Place where Savages Begin'.[25]

Thus ends the first third of the long course of the Changjiang. Still fast flowing, it cuts its way through the south of Sichuan, China's largest province, receiving four tributaries from the north-west (Sichuan means 'four rivers'). The volume of water varies greatly with the seasons. At Chongqing, the large river port in east Sichuan, the difference between 'high' and 'low' water levels is as much as 21m. The summer maximum of rain is augmented by vast snow-melt in the high mountains, causing tremendous problems for navigation along the only main east-west route in central China.

Sichuan, the size of France, with a population of 108 million (greater than that of Japan!) is unique in many ways. Known as the Red Basin on account of the fertile red sandstone which covers much of the area, it consists of undulating hilly country surrounded by high mountains, especially in the west, where the Azure Wall, or Sichuan Alps, reach Himalayan proportions, the highest peak Minya Gongga reaching 7556m. The general slope is to the south and east, the main entry being via the Yangtze Gorges beset with rapids and whirlpools, and for centuries navigable only during the periods between high and low water levels. The seasonal difference sometimes reached

[25]BBC Radio 4. 6 programmes 25.8.1992 to 29.9.1992.

46m as the summer surge raged through the bottle-neck of the gorges. The land route from Sichuan to the ancient centre of civilization in north China was by a series of 'plank' or 'trestle' roads, bamboo footpaths (with handrails) held to the mountainside by large timbers driven into the solid rock. Swing bridges of bamboo rope carried the paths across rivers and gorges. For centuries brick tea was exported along such a path to Tibet, via Batang. No wonder the great Tang poet Li Bai who lived for some years in Sichuan, wrote:

> The road to Sichuan
> Is harder than the road to Paradise.

In fact Sichuan was sometimes known as the 'Paradise on Earth'. In the words of an ancient record:

> Water comes and goes at man's will
> People have no idea of hunger,
> and there is no famine year
> This is the Land of Abundance.[26]

Edgar Snow, the well known American writer on Communist China, in his book *The Other Side of the River* has a chapter entitled 'Szechuan, "The Heavenly Land"' in which he comments: '. . . a simply fabulous land. If . . . separate . . . it might in itself be a world power. It has an extraordinary abundance of nearly all the resources required by a major nation.'[27] The climate is quite unusual for a region so far (1600km) from the sea. The encircling mountains keep out the bitter winds which freeze northern China in winter. Frost is almost unknown, but there is much cloud and mist. It is said that 'The dogs bark when the sun shines in Sichuan.' The name of the province to the south, Yunnan, means 'South of

---

[26]*Sichuan*, [Chengdu:] Sichuan People's Publishing House, 1985, quoted on p6.
[27]Edgar Snow, *The Other Side of the River*, Gollancz, 1963, Chap 76.

the clouds' and a city on the Changjiang, Yunyang, means 'Sun-clouded city'. The January temperature at Chengdu, the provincial capital, is 7°C, the same as that for Penzance in Cornwall, part of the 'English Riviera'. The combination of equable climate, reliable rainfall, fertile soil and varied altitude, has resulted in a growing period of 11 months, and therefore a great variety of crops. It has been said that anything which will grow in China can be grown in Sichuan, and much of the cultivated land is double cropped. Rice and wheat are the chief cereals, but maize is also grown. Many types of fruit flourish: oranges, native to the Changjiang valley, pears, plums, apricots, persimmons, lychees, even pineapples and bananas. Sugar cane is widely cultivated as are sweet potatoes, tea, mulberry trees for the silk industry, and bamboo, surely one of the most useful plants known to man. The variety of vegetables is almost endless, giving rise to the special Sichuan cuisine, famous throughout China, and now spreading to the rest of the world.

The man-made landscape of the province is one of the most beautiful to be found anywhere in the world. It has been said that 'The Chinese feeling for form has moulded the very fields of China.' The attitude of respect for Nature engendered by Daoism and the innate artistic talent shown throughout Chinese history in Neolithic pottery, Shang bronzes, and Ming porcelain, seems to have been instinctive in the peasant farmer, unlearned though he may have been. He cut his canals, divided his fields, and built his terraces up the hills with a feel for beauty, which has made the farming landscape a delight to the eye. Nowhere is this more evident than in the hilly country of east Sichuan where every hill is neatly contoured by terraced walls, the tiny fields extending to the top: where these are flooded for rice, the hillside becomes a so-called 'Shining Staircase'.

From a viewpoint on the main road from Chongqing to Beibei, and the North Hot Springs, the landscape of east Sichuan presents a mosaic of colours changing with the seasons: from the silver of the flooded rice terraces through the brilliant green of the young crop to the gold of harvest. The myriad greens of other crops and trees, and the clear yellow of flowering rape contrasting with scattered areas of rich red earth: the whole interspersed with shining pools of irrigation water linked by winding streams and small canals. A network of narrow footpaths (roads are a recent development in rural Sichuan) connects the farmsteads with their thatched roofs and surrounding trees, blending imperceptibly into the general scene.

A very different but equally beautiful man-made landscape exists in western Sichuan, in the area known as the Chengdu Plain. In the 1930s an American geographer abandoned his academic style to describe the area: '...one of the loveliest garden spots on earth ... nowhere in the world is there a more fertile, productive, or thickly populated agricultural area of similar size.'[28] Unlike the rest of Sichuan, the Chengdu Plain, a former lake basin, is flat, its green horizons lost in mist, long fading vistas broken only by the ghostly silhouettes of trees: a great sea of cultivation, its immaculate fields in all their variety of colour and texture, seen from the air to resemble nothing so much as a vast embroidered tapestry. For over 2000 years this wonderful 'garden spot' has been maintained without a break, helping to boost the food production of the 'Land of Abundance'.

The story began in 316 BC when Qin armies (who would later unify China for the first time) conquered the kingdoms of Shu and Ba (the future Sichuan).[29] An engineer named Li Bing, who had helped with city fortifications in the early days of the conquest, was appointed Governor in 250 BC. At that time the Chengdu Plain was almost useless for farming – a stony waste in the north and a marshy swamp in the south, owing to the seasonal ravages of the Min River. Emerging from the high mountains of the Azure Wall to the west, it was a quiet stream in winter, but a rushing torrent in summer,

---

[28]G.B. Cressey, *China's Geographic Foundations*, New York, 1934, quoted in E. Snow, ibid., p582.

[29]Joseph Needham, *Science and Civilization in China*, Vol IV, Part 3, Cambridge: CUP, 1971, p288–296, 'The Kuanhsien division-head and cut (Chhin)'.

bringing down a huge load of stones of all sizes, from boulders to gravel, and spreading them over the Plain as it flooded. Li Bing, assisted by his son Li Erlang, thought out an ingenious plan for controlling the river. He had the advantage of a strong system of government, with its ability to control large bodies of workers, and was helped by the seasonal rhythm of the Min's flow giving opportunities for hydraulic work during the period of low water. Also, unlike the Huanghe, it was silt free, and the ample supply of stones were to prove very useful for building dams and banks.

A plan was worked out to divide the river into two parts soon after it emerged from the mountains. The system became known as 'Dujiangyan' (the 'Dam on the Capital's River'). The main channel, on the west, would be left to drain southward to join the Changjiang as before, while the eastern half would be diverted to the Chengdu Plain, where it would be further divided and subdivided to provide a network of irrigation channels over the former lake basin. The stony area would be cleared so that cultivation would become possible. The small walled town of Guanxian ('Irrigation City') stood on a promontory tapering westward across the path of the proposed diversion, and Li Bing decided that a cut would have to be made through the solid rock, a hard conglomerate. It turned out to be a cut 40m deep and 27m wide, a colossal effort in those times. Li Bing was displaying the tremendous courage and initiative which has always been typical of the Chinese when faced with big environmental problems. They seem to have been willing to tackle almost anything in the days when the main resource available was human power. It is only in the past half-century that modern technology has been brought in. Enormous tasks, such as the attempt to control the Huanghe, the building of the Great Wall and the tomb of the First Emperor, the navigation of the treacherous Yangtze gorges, and the irrigation of the Chengdu Plain, to mention only a few of the countless projects undertaken, were tackled with consummate ingenuity, practical skill, and a refusal to face defeat seldom matched, and never exceeded, by the rest of mankind.

The famous rock-cut known as the 'Cornucopia Channel', or 'Mouth of the Precious Bottle' (Baopingkou) was assisted by the practice of lighting fires on or against the rock to stimulate cracking, a method known in many parts of the world. The main division head splitting the river into two parts was achieved by a barrier of piled stones, named the 'Fish Snout' from its shape. This was maintained in constant repair over more than 20 centuries. Various attempts were made to strengthen it. In the 13th century a giant iron tortoise weighing a tonne was placed in position, but was washed away in a summer surge. Six hundred years later two giant cast iron oxen (a total weight of 41 tonnes), with their heads joined together, but their tails separated were put in place, but they too were washed away. Centuries of experience have proved that the best defences against rushing water turned out to be large open-work 'baskets' or 'sausages' of strong bamboo fibre filled with stones. Various shapes and sizes of baskets and stones were used as required. The rush of water was dissipated among the stones, and the 'sausages' were not too heavy for the light soil. Stone revetments were often built round the 'fish snouts' at the various points of division, but though frequently renewed, they were never really successful. A certain amount of silting with gravel took place, and had to be cleared regularly. At one point a set of three iron bars each 3–4m long and weighing 0.6 tonne were fixed in the river bed to mark the correct level. Each year the bed was dredged until these bars appeared. Water levels had to be maintained and checked frequently. At one place a figure bears the inscription: 'In the dry season, let the feet be covered: in flood let the level not pass the waist.' The spillways, which led off surplus water at flood time, were very carefully constructed. The system of gauges, incorporating 8 water levels, was the work of Li Erlang, the son of Li Bing. At low water 60 per cent of the flow went through the Inner Channel, and 40 per cent through the Outer: at the flood season, vice-versa. Important instructions were cut into the rock at strategic points. Li Bing's watchword 'Dig the channels deep. Keep the dykes and spillways low', known as the 'Six Character Teaching' appears several times. This maxim, if it could have been followed on the Great Plain of north China, would have saved millions of lives. Li Bing and his son Li Erlang, became legendary figures, and temples were built to commemorate them. The one to Li Bing is at the top of Lidui (The Separated Hill) on the remnant of the promontory left by the Rock-cut. His son Li Erlang's temple is among the trees along the bank above the Rock-cut, and there cut in stone can be seen a summary of the instructions for maintaining the system, the 'Trimetrical Classic of River Control'. It is in a system of rhymed couplets, easy to memorise, based on a Confucian 'catechism' for schoolboys, used down to the 20th century.

From 'Trimetrical Primer – rhyming couplets for memorising':

> 'Dig the channel deep
> And keep the spillways low';
> This Six-Character Teaching
> Holds good for a thousand autumns.[30]
> Dredge out the river's stones
> And pile them on the embankments,
> Cut masonry to form 'fish snouts',[31]
> Place in position the 'sheep-folds',[32]
> Arrange rightly the spillways,[33]
> Maintain the overflow pipes in the small dams.[34]
> Let the bamboo (baskets) be tightly woven,[35]
> Let the stones be packed firmly within them.

---

[30]It has held good for over 2000 autumns!

[31]All the division heads: gabions are best, stones and iron less satisfactory, now concrete is used.

[32]Cylindrical gabions with parallel wooden slats, 10ft–20ft filled with stones (egg-sized).

[33]Gaps to let out the roaring billows.

[34]Such pipes placed at the bottom of small dams to prevent silting.

[35]Gabions: bamboo 'sausages' 10ft–20ft long: stone was tried, but it always failed. Gabions have two advantages: (i) water goes in and out slowly, (ii) they are not too heavy for the light soil. They were always used at Guanxian and the stone is still satisfactory in many parts of the works.

Divide (the waters) in the four-to-six proportion,[36]
Standardise the levels of high and low water
By the marks made on the measuring-scales;[37]
And to obviate floods and all disasters
Year by year dredge out the bottom
Till the iron bars clearly appear.
Respect the ancient system
And do not lightly modify it.

The famous Six-Character Teaching, referred to above, also appears in stone at the top of the main staircase of Li Erlang's Temple. Further up the hill is a beautiful little Daoist temple with the inscription:

The highest excellence does not lie in the highest place.
In changes and transformations let nothing be
contrary to Nature.

The maintenance of the system over the centuries has involved a strict annual cycle of work undertaken during the low water season, between October and March. The flow reaches its maximum in June and July 7500–10,000m^3 per second. It then declines; at first slowly, then faster during the autumn, reaching a minimum of 200–230m^3 per second by December. This persists until March, rising to 585m^3 per second in April, when the summer surge begins. The 'Fish Snout', the most important structure of all, was destroyed by floods and rebuilt many times. Recently it was reconstructed yet again with masonry rubble and cement mortar up to 5m above river level, and the foundations sunk to a similar distance below the river bed. Backed by the Diamond Dyke to the south, it forms a useful point from which to arrange the diversion of water for the annual clearing and repairs.

---

[36]Nei (Inner) Jiang at low water is 60%; Wai (Outer) Jiang is 40%; vice versa at flood times.
[37]The most important is in the Cornucopia channel (Baopingkou).

The work starts in mid-October, with the Outer Channel. The Inner Channel is dealt with in February and March, to be ready for the planting season in April. To divert the water, the ancient Chinese designed a unique temporary dam, known as 'matza'. Large wooden tripods (made from tree trunks about 7m long and 0.3m in diameter) were placed in a line across the channel, 50–60 for the Outer Channel, 60–70 for the Inner Channel, the upstream side faced with a mesh of poles and ropes, two layers of bamboo matting, and an 'apron' of packed clay. Other tripods were built out at right angles to break the force of the current. These were strengthened with the famous 'rock sausages' referred to earlier, which were also piled on wooden platforms half way up the main tripods to weigh them down securely. Repairs to the many small canals, dams and banks throughout the system were carried out at the same time as the major works. They also made extensive use of the 'rock sausages' thanks to the stones and boulders deposited by the Min, and the almost endless supply of bamboo. The ceremony known as the 'Opening of the Waters' took place traditionally in the first few days of April. It began with the selection of a Lucky Day by the water inspector, who then invited an official, the 'Intendant of Circuit', to come and perform the ceremony. If the Intendant felt that the day chosen was inauspicious he would select another. The Water Inspector then issued a proclamation to inform the people. On the day before the ceremony city officials met the Intendant and took him on a tour of inspection of the works, and afterwards to the residence where he would spend the night. While there he used the time to deal with some legal matters, such as complaints and disputes. A strange ritual followed in which the Water Inspector presented a feast to the Intendant, who politely refused it. It was then the turn of the local official to make the same offering, which was accepted. All the expenses of the occasion were borne by local officials, the Water Inspector playing only a small part.

On the next day, His Excellency the Intendant of Circuit rose before dawn, and visited the temple dedicated to the memory of Li Erlang, where he burned incense and made obeisance to the gods. He then went down to the river bank, where everything had been prepared for the ceremony. Incense and candles were already burning on a specially erected altar, and a pig and a goat had been sacrificed. Strong bamboo ropes had been attached to the tops of some of the tripods (matza), and several hundred coolies stood ready to pull them. A large crowd had assembled to watch the proceedings. At the moment of sunrise, His Excellency knelt down to worship the god of the river: the coolies gave a great shout and a tremendous pull. The barriers collapsed and the water rushed violently into the Inner Channel. Almost every year a few of the coolies were carried away and drowned in the onrush. His Excellency then presented a sum of money to be divided among the workmen and coolies, but it was not at his expense! As stated above the local officials had to pay for everything. His Excellency then departed for Chengdu, and quite often the water reached the capital first.

The water flows on into hundreds of kilometres of canals with all their branches, division heads and banks, meticulously maintained for over 2000 years. Many small bridges cross the channels but the 'King' of all the bridges is the bamboo suspension bridge, the An Lan, which links the two sides of the divided Min river just below the 'Fish Snout': 300m long, 8m high and 3m wide, for centuries it was a key link between Sichuan and the mountain people of Tibet. During the late Ming dynasty it was destroyed by fire, and for a time ferry boats were used. However in the 18th century, a teacher and his wife organized a fund to rebuild it, after which it became known as the 'Husband and Wife Bridge'. It was rebuilt in 1974, when the wooden piles were replaced by concrete and the bamboo ropes by steel cables.

Recently (1992) there has been a suggestion of reviving the ceremony of the Opening of the Waters as an attraction for visiting tourists and Chinese. The 'matza' have been replaced by electrically controlled sluice gates, and the diversions and water levels in the canals and spillways are managed from a central control room with a panel of press buttons, the first stage of the new system being completed in 1982. The irrigated area is being extended to the hilly country east of the Chengdu Plain by the building of a 6km tunnel through the Longquan Mountains, a trunk canal, and a new dam 53m high to hold back a reservoir retaining 300 million m^3 of water. The total irrigated areas is now $7300km^2$ and it is estimated that when all possible extensions have been completed it will amount to $17,800km^2$.

The Dujiangyan system has always done more than provide irrigation water. A stone tablet dating from the Yuan dynasty (1271–1368) states: 'Water-wheels for the milling and grinding of rice, for spinning and weaving machinery, to the number of tens of thousands, were established along the canals in the Plain of Chengdu, and operated throughout the four seasons.' Over 800 small power stations now generate electricity to replace these water-wheels.

The people of the Chengdu Plain, secure against the floods and droughts which beset so much of China, and enjoying their uniquely temperate climate, have always been amongst the most prosperous in the land. This is still true. As a result of the Responsibility System introduced in the late 1970s and early 1980s, numbers of well built two-storey houses are replacing the thatched farmsteads of the past. Sometimes a car can be seen parked outside, but the prosperity still has to be earned by hard work. In the first of her seminal series of books on China, *The Crippled Tree*, Han Suyin quotes from her father's diary for the year 1898. He writes:

> All day and half the night, bent over the fertile earth, the short thickset people of the plain, pale and stubby, worked the earth by hand, turned each mote of it by hand, plastered each ditch by hand, ploughed with men to pull the wooden plough, their feet and their legs sinking in the dung-thick, wet, oily soil. Carrying and planting, hoeing and banking, hauling water, treading the treadmill wheel, all day and half the night an enormous treadmill of toil went on by hand, by hand, all by hand.[38]

---

[38]Han Suyin, *The Crippled Tree*, London: Jonathan Cape, 1965, Chap 7, p91.

Chengdu, the capital of Sichuan, is a city over 2000 years old, steeped in history and legend. It became famous for its beautiful silk brocades, and was known as Jincheng, 'Brocade City'. A legend tells how a Buddhist monk accidentally fell into a dung heap and a lady of Chengdu offered to wash his robe. As soon as she dipped it into the water, the river miraculously filled with bright flowers. This was said to be the origin of the brocade industry.

In 145 BC the then Governor of Sichuan remarked that the people seemed ignorant and uncivilized, and therefore in need of education. He selected and trained a number of men, and sent them to the Imperial Capital to study. When they returned he put them in charge of a Department of Education, and sent out invitations to boys to come and study there. He took a personal interest in the scheme, taking students with him on his official visits, and giving them various privileges. Those who did well were able to obtain government positions, while the less able were awarded the title of 'Filially Instructed Farmer'. The general result of this project was a great increase in respect and desire for education by the general population: some rich people were prepared to pay for it. A writer 200 years later commented that the Governor's initiative had resulted in the province becoming a centre of culture and education. It also prompted the great Emperor Wu of the Han dynasty to establish government schools in the provinces.

After the fall of the Han dynasty in 220 AD, in the period known as the Three Kingdoms (220–280 AD) Chengdu, as the capital of Shu (formerly west Sichuan) was much involved in the struggle with Wu and Wei for the mastery of China. Memorial temples and tombs of outstanding heroes of that time such as Liu Bei (king of Shu) and his chief minister Zhuge Liang can still be seen in the southern parts of the city. A famous book the *Romance of the Three Kingdoms* records the battles and legends of those turbulent times. It became favourite reading for boys, and Mao Zedong once said that he and his boyhood friends read it many times, and could recount all the details of the stories. As a result of the enthusiasm for education, Chengdu became a centre for paper making and printing.

Indeed the world's oldest printed book, the 'Diamond Sutra' was printed in that city in 868 AD during the Tang dynasty.

The remoteness of Sichuan meant that it became a useful place of exile for those that who offended at the Imperial Court. Chengdu, with its culture and printing, often served also as a refuge for scholars and poets in times of upheaval. As the exiled officials usually were scholars, poets, or painters as well, Sichuan and its cities stood to gain as centres for art and literature. Du Fu, often regarded as the greatest of the Tang poets, came to Chengdu in 759 AD and stayed for four years, during which time he is reputed to have written 240 poems. His renovated thatched cottage is one of the tourist sights of modern Chengdu. Li Bai, almost equally famous, lived in the province from the age of five.

Bai Juyi, a third great Tang poet, was 'exiled' after disagreement at Court, and made governor of Zhongzhou, a city along the Yangtze in the east of Sichuan, in what was then known as Ba. At first he was at a town further east, but was later moved up the Gorges to Zhongzhou, much to his chagrin. He felt very isolated, and did not like the people: in various poems written at the time he complains:

How can I govern and lead these people aright?
I cannot even understand what they say

Among such as these I cannot hope for friends
And am pleased with anyone who is even remotely human.

They are people one meets, not people one cares for
At my front door guests also arrive
They are people one sits with, not people one knows.

He planted flowering trees on the 'eastern embankment' of the city, and was very disappointed that no one came to look at them. He wrote:

I simply bought whatever had most blooms,
Not caring whether peach, apricot, or plum.
A hundred fruits, all mixed up together;
A thousand branches, flowering in due rotation.

Each has its season coming early or late;
But to all alike the fertile soil is kind.
The red flowers hang like a heavy mist;
The white flowers gleam like a fall of snow.
The wandering bees cannot bear to leave them;
The sweet birds also come there to roost.
In front there flows an ever-running stream;
Beneath there is built a little flat terrace.
Sometimes I sweep the flagstones of the terrace;
Sometimes, in the wind, I raise my cup and drink.
The flower-branches screen my head from the sun;
The flower-buds fall down into my lap.
Alone drinking, alone singing my songs
I do not notice that the moon is level with the steps.
The people of Pa do not care for flowers;
All the spring no one has come to look.
But their Governor General, alone with his cup of wine,
Sits till evening and will not move from the place![39]

As centuries slipped away, Sichuan's remoteness preserved it from many of the upheavals and natural disasters which beset other areas, and in the final decades of the 19th century Chengdu and its fertile plain still basked in age-old security and charm. To this 'Paradise of fertility and beauty' as she called it, came a redoubtable woman traveller, Isabella Bird. Her account of her journey up the Yangtze and across Sichuan to Tibet makes fascinating reading, especially as a backdrop to modern travel. She set off in January 1896 accompanied by all the paraphernalia considered essential to the solitary, well-to-do, Victorian traveller venturing into far away places: personal servant, cook, letters of introduction, booking of accommodation, arrangements for hiring boats and sedan-chairs with their crews, trackers and carriers: these last arranged in advance by

[39]Arthur Waley, *Chinese Poems*, London: George Allen and Unwin, 1961, p150.

local British consuls and missionaries who occasionally accompanied her on some stages of the journey, and showed every consideration for her welfare, smoothing out difficulties with the 'natives' which occurred from time to time. However, this in no way detracts from her enthusiasm and courage in undertaking such an adventure: she constantly requested to be allowed to tackle things on her own, and on a number of occasions met a critical situation with calmness and humour.

She describes Chengdu as a handsome city surrounded by a 'noble wall 66ft wide at the base, 40ft at the top and 35ft high in admirable repair about 14 miles in circuit,' supported by an inner embankment almost the width of the wall, above which is a 'superb promenade' faced with very fine brick. Eight bastions are pierced by four fine gates. She says the streets are wide and well-paved, and refers to 'handsome shops', displaying fine filigree silverware and 'rich silk brocades gleaming in the shadows.' Richly dressed shopkeepers await customers and serve them with due dignity, but make no attempt to ensnare them. At the back of the shop there was always an image of the god of wealth, with an altar and incense.

She speaks of the splendour of officials, riding horses 'almost concealed' by expensive trappings, or carried in carved and gilded sedan chairs with poles raised high in the middle 'to raise the magnate above the heads of the plebeian herd.' She remarks that 'Chengdu owes nothing to Europe.'

The suburbs are 'charming, green and quiet, with beautiful gardens bright with flowers, and shady with orange and other fruit trees: ... tanks full of water plants ... goldfish ... the scent of tea roses floats on the sunny air: and all these groups of pleasant residences tell of affluent ease and the security in which it is enjoyed.'[40] An idyllic picture indeed! Sadly, the 'noble wall' has gone. Han Suyin's father in his diary, describes how the boys raced to the top to catch the first glimpse of the

[40]Isabella Bird, *The Yangtze Valley and Beyond*, London: Virago Press, 1985, reproduced from John Murray, 1899.

summit of Minya Gongga when it emerged from the mists of winter. It was, he says, visible on only a few spring days each year: '... this spring of 1898 we espied it, ... the shimmering triangular white peak of Miniaganka.'

Today Chengdu is a modern city of four million people, and an important industrial centre. The all-pervading cloud and mist, once clean and pure, is now polluted by industrial chemicals. Many of the commuting cyclists, who jam the streets during the rush hours, wear protective masks. Most of the new buildings, characteristic of the late 20th century, are similar to those of any great city in the world. In the rush to modern technology much has been lost. One is reminded of an African story in which a European explorer found that his porters were slowing down and falling behind. Their leader explained: 'Bwana, you go too fast for us; we must wait for our souls to catch up.' In time we hope they will. Department stores and buses have replaced the 'handsome shops' and gilded sedan-chairs described by Isabella Bird. She refers to six beautiful *pailou*, ornamental arches, erected across roads leading to important places along the road north from Chengdu. At least one is still standing, a sudden shock of ancient splendour for the tourists in the bus. In the back streets of the city one can sometimes glimpse the broken remains of an entrance arch with intricate carving, or a toppled wall; all that remains of a once beautiful courtyard house.

Deep beneath the fertile soil of Sichuan lie other treasures: deposits of coal, salt, natural gas and petroleum. For 2000 years drilling for brine has been carried on by ingenious methods. Men worked in shifts, jumping up and down off a heavy beam, while the drill bit was rotated by another man or men. Shifts lasted about 10 minutes, and were timed by the burning of incense sticks. The drill penetrated 0.6 or 1m in 24 hours, and it could take anything from 3 to 20 years to sink a well, the deepest of which went down 600m.[41] The same

[41]G.R.G. Worcester, *The Junkman Smiles*, Chatto and Windus, 1969, Chap 16, 'The Salt Wells of Tzeliutsing in Yentsingho'.

method was used 1000 years later, in the 12th century AD when the first artesian well in Europe was drilled, and in the USA where the early oil-men referred to the drilling as 'kicking her down'. For very large wells in China, teams of specially fed water buffaloes worked 10 shifts in 24 hours, involving 30 or more men at the same time. The brine was sometimes evaporated by pouring it over a hedge-like structure of dry thatch or thorn bushes, but where coal or natural gas were available these were used as fuel to boil the brine.

Natural gas and petroleum seeped through the ground, particularly in Sichuan, and further north in Gansu, where in the distant past the oil was used for greasing cart axles. In the 2nd century AD a book was written with the title *Record of the Investigations of Things* in which the writer describes a 'liquid ... fatty and sticky like the juice of meat.' He says 'it burns with an exceedingly bright flame.'[42] Nearly 1000 years later a famous astronomer and engineer collected the soot from burning oil to make ink, replacing the usual pinewood resin. He pointed out that the pine-woods were being used up so quickly that they would surely disappear in time, whereas 'petroleum is abundant, and more will be formed in the earth.' The inkmakers needed to be informed of the benefits of oil soot! It is interesting to notice references to deforestation in ancient China, as in Plato's time in Greece, the dangers of cutting down the forests were clearly recognised, though in the latter case it was for the building of ships rather than the manufacture of ink for the literati.

There is undoubtedly an aura of magic about Sichuan. Its richness and inaccessibility were legendary. The great mountain wall to the west marked the end of the known world to the ancient Chinese, for whom the earth was square and the heavens round. The Tang poet Du Fu wrote of 'A cloud in the wind at the corner of the world.' Somewhere, beyond the Azure Wall of mountains, was the signpost where the sun's

[42]Colin A. Ronan, *The Shorter Science and Civilization in China*, (Abridgement of Joseph Needham), Vol II, Cambridge: CUP, 1981, p295.

chariot turned away to resume its daily journey. Drawn by six dragons, it rose at dawn from the Pacific Ocean, lighting the top branches of the Heavenly Tree where Heaven's Cock crowed, giving the signal of sunrise to all the cocks on earth.

The two great rivers of China, the Huanghe and the Changjiang (Yangtze) begin in the Western mountains and flow eastwards to the Pacific Ocean. A poet of the Han dynasty wrote: 'The water in the rivers all eastward flow'; in other words, from the mysterious empty lands of mountain and desert, to the equally mysterious eastern ocean. There were legends of men being carried on rafts up moonlit rivers or out to sea, and finding themselves among the stars of the Milky Way. A fisherman reported seeing this happen every year in the eighth month on the east coast.[43] Du Fu has a line: 'Useless my mission adrift on the raft which came by this eighth month,' suggesting his failure to achieve his ambition to return to his duties in the capital.[44]

In the 19th century Sichuan, particularly the mountain areas, became a happy hunting-ground for botanists and plant collectors from Europe. They were amazed at the wonderful variety of species, some of which, like the 'Chinese fossil tree' (*metasequoia glyptostroboides*) had been considered extinct. It is now a protected species in China. Many varieties of rhododendrons, azaleas and other flowering shrubs, now fairly common in our parks and gardens, were brought here from Sichuan by enthusiastic plant hunters. An example of a rarer species, the lace bark pine, a beautiful tree found in Imperial gardens (a specimen can be seen in the garden in the Forbidden city) came to Kew Gardens through the efforts of a well known botanist, Robert Fortune.

Mount Emei, a place of pilgrimage, especially for Buddhists, is famous for its flowers, particularly rhododendrons. China

---

[43]Arthur Cooper, *Li Po and Tu Fu*, (Penguin Classics), Harmondsworth: Penguin, 1973, p65.

[44]A.C. Graham, *Poems of the Late Tang*, (Penguin Classics), Harmondsworth: Penguin, 1965, pp44, 52, 55.

now has almost 300 Nature Reserves, situated in many parts of the country where not only trees and flowers, but animals such as the giant panda, and birds, are protected.

The cuckoo is specially connected with Sichuan. A legend tells of a prince of Shu (ancient Sichuan) who was exiled, and was changed into a cuckoo so that he could return home each year, which he did in April, the third month of the lunar calendar. The song of the cuckoo sounds like the Chinese 'Go home!' so it became connected with exile and homesickness. A variety of azalea, also native to Sichuan, was known as the 'cuckoo flower'. The poet Li Bai, seeing these flowers when he was far from home, wrote a little poem (or song, as Tang poetry was set to music) entitled *On Seeing Cuckoo Flowers at Xuancheng*:

In Shu Land I have heard what the cuckoo calls,
At Hsüan-ch'eng I have seen the cuckoo flowers once more:
Let him call once, but once, at once my heart will break,
For the Spring thrice, Moon thrice, and thrice for San-pa![45]

In a comment, Arthur Cooper suggests the last line should be read: 'like Three cheers for Spring, and the Moon (third month) and San-pa (in Sichuan)' and that the whole poem, read in the original, echoes the cuckoo's call.

In September 1988, an Englishwoman working at the West China University of Medical Sciences at Chengdu, wrote a poem, *September in Chengdu*, which expressed in the first verse, the 'feel' of Sichuan – the misty warmth and the overcast sky seem to enhance the colours and scent of flowers, and the smell of damp earth and lush vegetation.

I walk to work through butterflies and dragon flies
The air is still: mist hazes the upturned roofs,
Sullen cloud sits heavily overhead,

---

[45]Arthur Cooper, *Li Po and Tu Fu*, (Penguin Classics), Harmondsworth: Penguin, 1973, p155.

Rarely does the sun shine:
But the marigolds glow
And the salvias flame
And I walk to work through butterflies and dragonflies.

The end lines of the last verse read:

And hedged around by a blaze of scarlet and gold
Transported, elevated,
I walk to work through butterflies and dragonflies.[46]

In spite of the loss of so much former beauty, the rush hours, and the pollution, it seems that the ancient magic still works.

[46]Betty Walker, in *Quaker Monthly*, September 1988.

4

DOWN THE LONG RIVER II
The Yangtze Gorges

'The road to Sichuan is harder than the road to Paradise' was no less true of the only possible waterway to the province than it was of the land route via the terrifying 'trestle roads' from the north. The journey through the gorges between Yichang and Chongqing, the chief river port of Sichuan, was described thus: 'The 350 mile journey ... is most hazardous, and probably contains more navigational risks and difficulties than any river in the world.'[47] This from a former River Inspector with long experience working for the Chinese Maritime Customs during the first half of this century. He also states that in his time, the greatest threat to navigation on the upper Yangtze was the rapids, of which there were 72 within 150 miles of Yichang.

There were two main reasons for these hazards, the first was the difference in water level between the seasons: as mentioned earlier, this was 21m at Chongqing, where the mud slopes of the winter 'low' were used by the poor for temporary housing and quick crops. Further east, the seasonal levels vary as the valley opens out or closes in where the pent-up river plunges through the famous 'Three Gorges'. At Wanxian, just before the Qutang gorge the difference is 33m reaching 60m in the Wushan gorge, and at Wuhan out on the flat plain beyond the gorges, it is still 15m. This had to be allowed for when the first great road and rail bridge across the Yangtze was built. It was

[47]G.R.G. Worcester, *Sail and Sweep in China*, London: HMSO, 1966, p105.

opened in October 1957. Riverside towns have always been placed high above maximum levels, with flights of steps down to 'low' water, and floating wharves and landing stages.

Secondly, the profile of the river-bed through the gorges is not the normal smooth 'curve of water erosion' typical of most rivers. It has been shown that when large bodies of water are forced through a narrow gap, there is uneven erosion of the river bed.[48] This is clearly demonstrated in the Yangtze gorges. The bottom of the channel between Chongqing and Wanxian, a distance of about 160km slopes fairly evenly from about 120m to 90m above sea-level, with two 'dips' down to 60m, but in the Wushan gorge it is actually below sea-level for a short distance. After this for the next 80km the highest points average 30–45m above sea-level with at least nine 'dips' to below 15m.[49] A navigable channel about 2.75m deep well marked by buoys, has now been blasted out along the whole course, but in the past many rocks protruded or were dangerously submerged, according to the season. The effect was that the river, already squeezed into a narrow channel, was flowing up- and down-hill along the uneven bed, creating rapids, whirlpools and eddies on a huge scale. Even in the 1970s these still looked menacing, whirling circles of water being sucked down through a central 'hole', rather like a huge bath plug. These eddies were sometimes several hundred feet across. The surface of the river swells and heaves, as if it were alive. No wonder that the Chinese believed that down below a great dragon was forever lashing its tail!

The scenic splendour of the gorges is partly the result of the great variety of rocks encountered by the river. The three main gorges, Qutang, Wushan or Wu, and Xiling, occur where the river has cut deeply into exposures of limestone. Here vertical rock walls rise 300m or more on each side of narrow clefts

---

[48]George B. Barbour, 'Physiographic history of the Yangtze', *Geographical Journal*, 1936, Vol 87, p17–34.

[49]Ibid. p25–6; quoting from S.C. Plant, *Handbook for Guidance of Shipmasters*, Shanghai, 1932, p5.

where the water surges and eddies, or foams over rapids. Between the gorges the valley opens out, revealing the colours and textures of granite, sandstone, shales and slates. On south-facing slopes, open to the sun, flights of terraces meticulously cultivated with vegetables, tea bushes, and orange and tung-oil trees display the ingenuity of the Chinese farmer in adapting to an almost vertical lifestyle. Philip Short of the BBC noted in 1992 that it took 100 men two days to complete a terrace.[50] Irrigation of these terraces depends on a complicated arrangement of ropes, pulleys, and buckets to raise water from the river.

Even in these more open sections, higher peaks loom in the background, enhancing the closed-in, world-of-its-own atmosphere of the valley between Chongqing and Yichang. Ancient cities, small towns and villages, rich in history and legend, seem to belong only to the river, clinging mainly to the south-facing bank, linked by a myriad of small boats carrying people and local produce to market and children to school; back and forth, keeping to the calmer water near the banks. Life is two-dimensional; vertical up and down the mountain-sides, horizontal along the river. Up and over the top of the 300m cliffs is almost 'terra incognita'. A recent expedition in search of 'gigantopithecus' a possible survival of a primitive type of man said to have been seen by many local people in the mountains north of Wanxian, found themselves in wild forested country as remote from the riverside life as it was from the cities of modern China.

Although due attention was paid to the *feng-shui* of the sites when most towns and cities were founded, some turned out to be more fortunate than others. Wanxian, for example, has seemed to have everything in its favour. Shielded by a range of hills to the north from unlucky 'Yin' influences, it is open to the south from whence comes light and good fortune (Yang), and a fine rock, known at one time as 'The Celestial City' rises 360m above the walls. Archibald Little described a three-storied

[50]BBC Radio 4. 6 programmes 25.8.1992 to 29.9.1992.

pavilion on the river bank, and two pagodas on points jutting out below the town.[51] Most towns along the Yangtze had pagodas on the down-river banks, to prevent good fortune being swept away by the river. Wanxian has the advantage of being in a right-angled bend in the river, which means that the city looks down two reaches, to the south and east. In the 19th century it was a rich and prosperous city, inhabited by well-to-do families who chose to live there because of the security of the site. The surrounding countryside was famous for its wealth of refuges, hilltop sites to which people fled in times of war or rebellion. Wanxian was well-known for its junk-building, using the tough cypress wood of local trees. Isabella Bird describes a beautiful house used by the China Inland Mission: it had once belonged to a mandarin. She too was impressed by the wealth of Wanxian. In 1979 all this had deteriorated and the street above the river was full of pot-holes.

By way of contrast Badong in the 19th century was described by Little as 'the poorest district city of the province.'[52] The surrounding country was wild and desolate, with very little cultivation. He says that the *feng-shui* was very defective, but following the building of a tall white six-stored pagoda a mile below the town things had improved somewhat and just before his visit the town had produced its first graduate for 200 years in the Imperial examinations! The only trade seemed to be a small production of coal.

The great river port of Chongqing is easily the most important city on the upper Yangtze. The settlement, on a rocky peninsula at the junction of the Yangtze and Jialing, dates back 4000 years. At one time it was the capital of the ancient kingdom of Ba, and during the war with Japan (1938–1945) it served as the capital of Nationalist (Guomindang) China. The city now has a population of 13 million if surrounding suburbs are included, of which two million are in the actual city.

---

[51]Archibald Little, *Through the Yang-Tse Gorges*, London: Sampson Low and Co, 1888.
[52]Ibid.

Over the centuries Chongqing has suffered consistently from a lack of space. Hemmed in by the rivers on south, east, and north, expansion was only possible to the west, and this became blocked by the ever-growing city cemetery. Archibald Little comments that 'the dead have more space than the living in eastern Szechuan.' The streets were narrow and steep, with many steps, more than 200 from the highest point to the water level. The pavements, supported by stone walls and paved with limestone slabs, were built on the accumulated debris of centuries. No wheeled vehicles were allowed within the city walls until 1927, and even in 1979 a party of tourists were taken round in taxis as the streets were too steep to accommodate their coach.

A century ago there were many fine houses and 'hongs' (business premises) in the upper part of the city belonging to prosperous merchants. The poor were packed on the lower slopes, from whence they spread on to the muddy foreshore during the winter low-water level. Owing to the seasonal rise and fall of 20m or more fixed wharves were an impossibility, and landing stages, as elsewhere on the Upper Yangtze were (and still are) floating pontoons.

Modernization began in the 1930s, but was held up by the Japanese war of 1938–1945, when the city suffered extensive bomb damage. Since 1945, however there has been considerable expansion as Chongqing grew along the Jialing, and to a large extent on the opposite bank of the Yangtze. The completion of the long-awaited bridge in the early 1980s will no doubt lead to great developments there.

Although the local climate, with its excessively hot humid summers (it has been nicknamed 'The Furnace of the Yangtze'), and the ever present Sichuan fog, now often contaminated by industrial 'smog', is hardly conducive to tourism, Chongqing is nevertheless well worth a visit, as an example of a great modern Chinese city. Though its ancient walls and buildings have gone, the old city with its steep narrow streets and endless steps is still fascinating; the newer parts are pleasantly laid out with trees and flowers and public parks: there is a fine art centre, an interesting museum, and theatres where ancient Sichuan operas are still performed: not to mention the many restaurants specializing in the local spicy cuisine. Above all the excellent communications make Chongqing a fine centre from which to explore the beauty of Sichuan, and the soon-to-vanish gorges.

The dangerous passage through the gorges has led, over the centuries, to a proliferation of legends and superstitions. As so often in the past, natural dangers were compounded by the fears of the supernatural, but this was somewhat mitigated by belief in beneficent influences, whose aid could be called upon. Many caves in the limestone were thought to be the homes of dragons, and often chains were fixed across the entrances to protect passing travellers. One cave near Fengdu was regarded as the entrance to Hell, a result of so-called 'fire wells' nearby. These were caused by emanations of natural gas, which ignited from time to time. Added to the pagodas referred to above, which though Buddhist in origin were mainly connected with *feng-shui*, Daoist and Buddhist monasteries occupied many hilltops. 'Fairy Girl Peak' in the Wu gorge, was the home of a goddess who looked after navigators. Statues of the Buddha were placed at dangerous points along the course, sometimes on rocks in midstream, where passing junkmasters would pause to pay their respects and burn incense. Three kilometres above Fengdu there was a Buddha-head mounted on a spur of rock: when the water rose over the head the junkmen tackled the nearby rapid at their own risk, and so long as the water was over the mouth the Buddha could not warn them. Only when the whole head appeared could they believe that the rapid was safe. A legend tells of a monastery near Fuling where grain production was difficult. A miraculous supply of rice appeared whenever a priest put a handful of rice in a hole in the floor, but the supply ran out when a wicked monk enlarged the hole. Later however, the gods fertilized the local soil so that the monks could produce enough for their needs.

Legend melts into history in places where ancient objects or buildings can be identified, such as the area round Baidi, near the western entrance to the Qutang gorge. Baidi ('White

Emperor's City') is known to have been the site of a fortress almost 2000 years ago. It is in an excellent strategic position, with water on three sides, and mountains behind. In the local museum are axes, spears and swords dating back to Shang and Zhou times, seventeen to eleven centuries BC. Two fine bronze swords from the time of the Warring States (475–221 BC) have also been found. The city was founded in 25 BC by a local ruler, Gongsun Shu, who had hoped to become master of central China, but was defeated and killed in battle. The temple built in his memory, and restored during the 16th century, still dominates the hill-top. Baidi also played an important part in the struggle recorded in the *Romance of the Three Kingdoms* in the 3rd century AD. Liu Bei, king of Shu, made it his base. After his defeat by the army of Wei he retreated to Baidi and died there in 223 AD, leaving the care of the city and his son in the hands of his prime minister, Zhuge Liang, who was renowned for his wisdom and military strategy. Dating from these times also is a feature on the right (south) bank of the river known as 'Mengliang's Ladder'. It consists of a number of square holes, each 36cm square penetrating 0.6m into the cliff. Wooden beams were inserted into these holes to enable Mengliang's soldiers to ascend and descend the vertical rock-face. The narrowest part of the entrance to the gorge is a mere 135m wide, and at one time there was an iron chain across the river. Two iron pillars remain from several pairs which were put in place in 1264 AD. These were linked by seven iron chains each 90m long, which were strung across the river. Further east, at the western end of the Xiling gorge, the small city of Zigui was one of the ancient capitals of the state of Chu, one of the cradles of Chinese civilization, and home of the famous poet Qu Yuan, who lived in the 3rd century BC.

The necessity to keep in touch with the riches of the 'Land of Abundance' in spite of the difficulties of access by land and water posed a great challenge to Chinese courage and ingenuity. It has taken 20 centuries for safe travel to be accomplished. Only in the last hundred years have adequate roads, railways and navigation through the gorges been achieved.

Yang Tai, a pirate of the Upper Yangtze who became a junkmen's god, and who lived in the 12th century AD is reported to have said that the government could never capture his fastness 'unless they could fly and come from the air'.[53] Eight centuries were to pass before the traveller could enjoy the magical experience of dropping down through the Sichuan fog to tantalising glimpses of lush farmland and rich forest, a secret foretaste of the beauty to be revealed later.

Archibald Little wrote that he rejoiced at his good fortune 'to visit the gorges before the inevitable steamboat and the omnivorous globe-trotter destroy their charm.'[54] However, this did not deter him from introducing, and piloting, the first steamboat (the *Leechuan*) to make the journey in 1900! He could not foresee that almost a century later, the Chinese themselves would be contemplating building a huge dam which would not only silence the fearsome river for ever, but would create a huge lake in the gorges, drowning much of the splendid scenery, and many ancient cities.

The hazards to navigation have already been described, the dramatic seasonal changes in water level being among the worst. In Tang times the route was closed for five months each year. The poet Bai Juyi mentions this when he was sent to Sichuan in 819 AD:

Henceforward – relegated to deep seclusion
In a bottomless gorge, flanked by precipitous mountains.
Five months on end the passage of boats is stopped
By the piled billows that toss and leap like colts.[55]

By the 19th century this had decreased to three months: June, July and August. There was always danger, from sudden freshets in early summer as the snows melted, and the gradual

---

[53]G.R.G. Worcester, *Sail and Sweep in China*, London: HMSO, 1966, p107.
[54]Archibald Little, *Through the Yang-Tse Gorges*, London: Sampson Low and Co, 1888.
[55]Arthur Waley, *Chinese Poems*, London: George Allen and Unwin, 1961, p150.

reappearance of submerged rocks in the autumn. Anchors could not be used on the large junks mooring for the night, as the river could rise or fall by 6ft or 7ft (1.8m or 2m) in as many hours. The pilots and junkmasters (known as *laoda* meaning 'Old Great') were the élite of the Upper Yangtze, their great skill and expertise in the details of the river being handed down from father to son through many generations. Even so, each pilot trained for five years. In the words of G.R.G. Worcester 'finer seamen would be hard to find than those who man the junks of the Upper Yangtse'.[56] Two winds helped or hindered the difficult passage through the gorges: the prevalent up-river wind blowing from September to May, and the more variable down-river wind of the summer. The wind was seldom felt in some of the narrower reaches where oars or trackers were used, and where the junkmen sometimes followed the ancient practice of whistling for the wind, or engaged in noisy rituals to gain the co-operation of the relevant gods.

Before the steam engine solved the problem of the up-river passage, the Chinese used their only resource, man power. Teams of 'trackers', sometimes numbering several hundred men, were hired to pull the junks upstream against the strong current. In some places trackers' paths were cut into the cliffs of the river bank, but often the men had to scramble over rocks. They wore a harness which was attached to a tow-rope made from strips of bamboo, lighter and more durable than hemp. These bamboo ropes could be up to 400m long, and were carried in enormous coils on the junk's foredeck. In an emergency the men could disconnect themselves instantly, to avoid being thrown on the rocks or into a rapid. Even so quite a number were drowned or injured. As the average loss of junks was about ten percent the same applied to the junk crews. Isabella Bird records seeing down-river junks carried onto rocks, and exploding as if blown up to disappear completely, disintegrating into a thousand fragments. The up-river

[56]G.R.G. Worcester, *Sail and Sweep in China*, London: HMSO, 1966, p113.

journey could take up to 50 or 60 days, with an average speed of less than 3km per hour; but down-river from Chongqing to Yichang could be completed in 5 to 12 days – a headlong rush 'shooting' the rapids, the masts shipped alongside to act as fenders, and on a large junk, a crew of 50 men manning the oars and yulohs (sculling oars) and struggling with the great bowsweep to keep the junk in the axis of the stream, and avoid collisions with those travelling in the opposite direction. The poet Li Bai wrote in *Early Departures from White King City* (i.e. Baidi):

At dawn we leave White King,
  its clouds all coloured,
For passage to Kiang-ling[57]
  in one sun's circuit:

While both banks' gibbons cry
  calls still unceasing,
Our light boat has gone by
  many fold mountains.

Arthur Waley notes that there were true reports of such a down-stream journey being completed in 24 hours.[58]

In some places where there was no wind, or tracking was impossible, the only way to proceed up stream was by rowing or 'clawing' the junk along by bamboo poles tipped with metal hooks, using iron rings which had been attached to the rock face. The junk was fended off the rocks by poles with metal spikes, which were also used, where possible to 'punt' her along. Behind the trackers a small group of strong swimmers, were ready at any moment to plunge into the river and disentangle the tow-rope from any obstacle which may have fouled it.

The life of the trackers was one of unremitting physical toil.

[57]320km distant.
[58]Arthur Cooper, *Li Po and Tu Fu*, (Penguin Classics), Harmondsworth: Penguin, 1973, p116.

They worked from sunrise to sunset, straining at the tow ropes, often bent double, slipping and scrambling over the rocks, their movements controlled by a drum-beat from the junk signalling 'Stop', 'Slow', or 'Fast'. They received low wages and their food, three meals a day of rice, beans, and cabbage, plus a little chicken or fish occasionally. They endured this hard life with courage, patience, and a sense of humour which elicited the admiration of travellers like Isabella Bird and Archibald Little, and river officials such as G.R.G. Worcester.

Han Suyin quotes from her mother's diary:

> ... I have never seen anything so wonderful. It was not like sailing at all, it was climbing, climbing a mountain of water which came rushing at us, and that is how the boatmen spoke of it, as pushing up against the Great River. Most of the time we were being towed, up up up against the current, ... the boatmen were fighting, all the time, every step of the way; the towmen and the boatmen, all through these two and a half months, fought for our lives on that junk, ... You will never know what it is like to fight for your life through the gorges if you go by steamer.[59]

Certain rituals always preceded the beginning of a journey. A sacrificial cock was killed, and its blood sprinkled in certain places on the bow and each side of the junk, and some feathers stuck with blood, on the side of the great bow sweep, and the fore part of the deck house. Incense was burned, and firecrackers let off. The pilot or *laoda* who had performed this ceremony then folded his hands and kowtowed to north, south, east, and west. A few grains of rice were picked by chopsticks, placed in a bowl of water, and poured into the river as a libation to the gods. The pilot, specially engaged to take the junk through bad rapids, then took his place on a plank in the stern, giving him a clear view of the river ahead. He then 'read the water', raised his hand, and proceeded to

---

[59]Han Suyin, *The Crippled Tree*, Jonathan Cape, 1965, p294.

signal with his index finger. The *laoda* standing beside him, manipulated the 4.5m long tiller in accordance with the signals, as did the men in charge of the bow sweep. Also standing beside the pilot was the drummer who controlled the trackers.

The journey through the gorges was always dreaded by officials posted to Sichuan, and in 819 AD the Tang poet, Bai Juyi, summed up the general feeling in the following poem entitled *Alarm at first entering the Yang-tze Gorges*:

> Above, a mountain ten thousand feet high;
> Below, a river a thousand fathoms deep.
> A strip of sky, walled by cliffs of stone;
> Wide enough for the passage of a single reed.
> At Chü-t'ang a straight cleft yawns;
> At Yen-yü islands block the stream.
> Long before night the walls are black with dusk;
> Without wind white waves rise.
> The big rocks are like a flat sword;
> The little rocks resemble ivory tusks.
>
> We are stuck fast and cannot move a step.
> How much the less, three hundred miles?
> Frail and slender, the twisted-bamboo rope;
> Weak, the treacherous hold of the punters' feet.
> A single slip – the whole convoy lost;
> And *my* life hangs on *this* thread!
> I have heard a saying 'He that has an upright heart
> Shall walk scatheless through the lands of Man and Mo.'[60]
> How can I believe that since the world began
> In every shipwreck none have drowned but rogues?
> And how can I, born in evil days
> And fresh from failure, ask a kindness of Fate?
> Often I fear that these un-talented limbs
> Will be laid at last in an un-named grave![61]

---

[60]Man and Mo = savages.

[61]Arthur Waley, *Chinese Poems*, London: George Allen and Unwin, 1961, p149.

The great poet Du Fu, in *Down the Great River to Dongting* expresses similar feelings:

> Evil rapids! How can one not change colour?
> . . .
> Books of poems, histories, all are overturned, scattered,
> Travelling bags, packs, half are crushed, drenched,
> On precipice of life, I look down, giddy, anxious
> A place of death we may reach at any instant.[62]

Shipbuilding has a long history in China. Rivers and canals were used for transport from the earliest times. The navigation of the Huanghe and the Upper Yangtze offered a special challenge, while the calmer waters of the many lakes and lowland rivers were an excellent training ground for sailing and boat-building. The famous Grand Canal linking the fertile lands of the lower Yangtze to the northern capital, was built to facilitate the movement of huge quantities of rice and other foodstuffs from south to north. Boats were adapted to 'sail' on the 'sea' of mud which bordered the shrunken Lake Dongting during the dry season, and flat-bottomed junks were hauled across the surface by water-buffalo. On the frozen rivers and canals of the North, boats were fitted with sledge runners and in the absence of wind were propelled across the ice by men using long pointed metal staves. They worked in shifts, timed by the burning of incense sticks. This is graphically described by an American traveller in the 1920s, who was taken in a family boat on the frozen Grand Canal, which was alive with all kinds of traffic, including many skaters.[63]

Officials touring their provinces often travelled by special boats known as mandarin house boats. At one time there was an exquisite small model of one of these in the Chinese Junk Section of the Science Museum in London's South Kensington.

---

[62] *Tu Fu: The Autobiography of a Chinese Poet, A.D. 712–770*, Vol 2: *Travels of a Chinese Poet*, trans. Florence Ayscough, London: Jonathan Cape, 1929.
[63] Nora Waln, *The House of Exile*, London: Cresset Press, 1944.

Later it disappeared, one hopes only temporarily. These boats were obviously suitable only for calm waters, and were often luxuriously furnished, and carried a full compliment of servants and everything else deemed necessary for a mandarin's life-style. The model in the Museum closely resembled the famous Marble Boat at the Summer Palace in Beijing, built in the 1880s by the Dowager Empress, using funds originally intended for the Chinese Navy. This is said by some to be the cause of the Chinese defeat in the war with Japan in 1894–1895. The Empress used the boat for elaborate banquets and entertainments. She also liked to go fishing on the Lake Kunming. Such was her arrogance if she was unsuccessful, that her servants were said to have dived in and attached a large fish to her line to keep Her Majesty in a good mood.

To return to the Upper Yangtze: all the skill of the Chinese boatbuilders was needed to cope with the difficulties of the rapids and the narrow twisting courses of some of the tributaries. One remarkable result was the crooked-stern junk of the former Fuling river (now the Wujiang). These were built at Fuzhou (now renamed Fuling), and Isabella Bird records that on first sight of such a junk she assumed that it had been involved in a severe accident! Later she saw a number stacked together, each with its stern twisted 'a quarter round' and describes the sight as 'absolutely laughable'.[64]

The origin of the crooked-stern junk is lost in legend, though G.R.G. Worcester thinks that it was the result of hundreds of years of trial and error, resulting in a design remarkably suited to its purpose. The town of Fuling, at the junction of the Wujiang and the Yangtze had a bad reputation, like most of Sichuan, for smuggling, banditry, and opium-dealing and it was said that most of its inhabitants could not see straight, and even the junks had crooked sterns.

The legendary origin concerns the carpenter god Lupan, and a retired dragon who had too little to do, as there could not

---

[64]Isabella Bird, *The Yangtze Valley and Beyond*, London: Virago Press, 1985, reproduced from John Murray, 1899, p491–2.

possibly be any junk traffic on so difficult a river. Lupan devised the crooked stern junk, which because of its strange shape would be able to tackle the worst rapids on the river, and thereby provide suitable work for the dragon in looking after the sailors. He is said to have observed a hawk 'banking', and based the design of the crooked stern on the arrangement of its tail feathers. Another story tells how the dragon challenged Lupan to build a wooden pagoda with no nails, which he did and the dragon agreed to allow more junks on the river. The twisted stern makes possible the use of two sweeps, one larger than the other, instead of a rudder: as they work in parallel, they cannot foul each other. For anyone interested, full details of the construction of this extraordinary boat are given in G.R.G. Worcester's fascinating book,[65] which also includes the remarkable story attached to the model of the crooked stern junk on show at the Science Museum in London. This replica, on a scale of one inch to one foot, was made at Fuling during World War II, by two men who were actually engaged in building a crooked-stern junk. Both the junk and the model were completed in two weeks. As the junk builders have always worked without plans but from knowledge handed down through generations from father to son, the two men had never heard of scale models, and were given cardboard patterns of the various parts. The model is 2m long, and the smallest details are represented down to the cooking stove, the bamboo ropes, and even the trackers' harness. It was launched at a special ceremony, complete with the ritual of the killing of a cock and the fixing of feathers to the correct points on the junk, in the presence of town dignitaries. This was followed by a procession to the steamer, which was to take it to Chongqing. On the way it narrowly escaped destruction from Japanese bombs during a severe air-raid. It was then flown to Hong Kong and Shanghai. In December 1941, the Japanese took over the International Settlement at Shanghai. To prevent its confiscation the model was wrapped in a

[65]G.R.G. Worcester, *Sail and Sweep in China*, London: HMSO, 1966, p125.

blanket in a large box and buried secretly in the garden of the Customs Reference Library. At the end of the war it was dug up, and found to be in perfect condition. It was brought to England in a troopship carrying freed prisoners of war. To quote Worcester 'Having covered 14,000 miles by rail, sea, and air, it has found an honourable place in the Science Museum.' Well worth making an effort to see it!

Other remarkable junks on this part of the river included the famous salt boats designed with crooked bows, which were probably in use for 1700 years. Another was a two-section junk which could quickly be divided into two for negotiating sharp bends on a narrow river. A third was a type of wupan, built at Chongqing of old wood and made to last one journey only. It was used for mail, and any passengers prepared to take the risk of the down-river rush. When it arrived at Yichang it was broken up for firewood, after a journey taking only three or four days, or on one record occasion 2 days 15 hours, to complete.

Later on the scene, in the mid 19th century, came the famous Red Lifeboats of the Upper Yangtze, started by a rich merchant who collected money from traders and built three special boats for rescue work, which became known as the 'Dare to Die' service. Well-wishers added more boats from time to time, and in 1883 came government recognition and the founding of the Life Saving Office. In 1889 the Red Boats saved 1473 lives from 49 wrecked junks. By now the service was very well organized, with the river divided into districts, and every up-river junk going through a rapid was accompanied by a Red Boat. By the 1940s this excellent enterprise had been allowed to lapse.[66] The Chinese contribution to shipbuilding has been unique. The square sterns of their junks, in contrast to the curved sterns of Western ships, made possible the development of the stern-post rudder which was in general use in China by the 4th century AD, but did not reach Europe for another 800 years. Many different designs were

[66]Ibid. p122–129.

used in China, according to circumstances. Chinese anchors and sails were also unique, as was their invention of watertight compartments in the holds of ships. Last, but by no means least came the mariner's compass. Junk building on the Yangtze was greatly helped by the presence of suitable timber, mainly cypress and pine, and by the well-known tung oil tree, whose oil is known as the best drying and waterproofing vegetable oil in existence. It has been used for centuries in China for proofing and preserving wood, paper (including umbrellas), cloth, basketwork, and even masonry. It can also be burned in lamps. Sichuan is the main producer, where the tree grows on hillsides between 200 and 2000m and needs minimum attention. Most farmers own a few trees, and in the 1920s and 1930s it was the chief export of China. It is used in the USA for varnish and enamel and for brake linings. It dries with a high gloss which gives the boats an attractive finish and is resistant to water, acid and cracking. The seeds are roasted, ground to powder, and pressed to release the oil.[67]

Only by a strange quirk of history did the great ocean voyages of Admiral Zheng He in the 15th century fail to achieve the rounding of the Cape of Good Hope before Vasco da Gama reached India from Portugal. A new Emperor had decided that long voyages were a waste of money, and refused to sponsor any more, though a considerable trade had developed with East Africa. Large quantities of Chinese porcelain have been dug up near Mombasa, of which some interesting examples are displayed in the museum at Fort Jesus.

The pace of change has accelerated dramatically and by 1979 when the author travelled through the gorges from Chongqing to Wuhan on a passenger boat, the life and activity on the great river, as described in G.R.G. Worcester's book published in 1966, had almost completely vanished. The cry of the gibbons calling across the river from the forests, so evocative of emotion for homesick poets and officials in the past, could

[67]G.F. Deasy, 'Tung oil production and trade', *Economic Geography*, 1940, No 260.

no longer be heard. Gone too were the great junks and the turmoil described by 19th century travellers, the din of the drums and gongs, and the yelling of the trackers, and above all the roar of the rapids, but the river still showed its power as it swirled and eddied towards the sea, appearing often to race ahead of the boat. In place of junks, steam or motorized barges sometimes linked two or three together, carried cargoes of coal, timber, or stone, but nearer the banks and in calmer water, smaller traditional junks and sampans plied back and forth, using their flat sails or oars, and sweeps the size of telegraph poles. The up-river wind was blowing strongly in late September and it was interesting to note in some places small settlements where each building had its 'back' to the wind with all doors and windows on the leeward side.

The passenger boat of 1979, *The East is Red 46* had been built in 1977 for the Yangtze River Shipping Company. It was one of a fleet of similar ships used on the river between Shanghai and Chongqing for passengers as well as freight, from which the main profit was made. Our party of 24 were the first Europeans to sail on her, and as such, we enjoyed favoured treatment. In recent years, special cruise ships have been built for the use of tourists. These are luxuriously fitted out, but it was certainly more interesting to be on a 'normal' Chinese ship. We shared the first class accommodation with a party of Japanese tourists, and a few 'high status' Chinese. One evening we were invited to a session with some of the crew, and given interesting details about the running of the ship. The crew numbered 90, and consisted of 60 men and 30 women, all of whom had family connections along the route. There were three types of work: steering, engineering and service (food and rooms) arranged in three shifts of eight hours each. One shift consisted of four hours work followed by eight hours rest, followed by four hours work. The usual trip was a return between Shanghai and Wuhan or Wuhan and Chongqing each taking eight days, though sometimes it was the whole length Shanghai to Chongqing. Work was continuous, with no Sundays off, but was followed by a sixty day holiday each year, taken all at once. Wages varied between 40 and 200 yuan per month, plus food. (1980 exchange rate £1 = Y3.3, but these figures have very little meaning, owing to the very different commodity prices and lifestyle.) Sunday work earned double pay. All the crew were members of a Trade Union, whose function was mainly concerned with health and welfare, rather than pay-bargaining. There was a rule forbidding marriage before the age of 25. If a crew member became ill, full wages were paid for six months and 70 per cent after that. In the event of an accident preventing further work, full wages were paid until death. Men retired at 60 and women at 55 on a pension which could be increased by voluntary further work. A crew member who had achieved the title of 'Labour Hero or Heroine' retired on full salary. A typical member was a young woman aged 18. She had graduated from Senior Middle School, spent two years in the countryside (compulsory at that time, but no longer so) and attended an engineering school. We had the impression of a happy ship. The crew seemed healthy and well-turned out, and there was a pleasant area of foredeck decorated with potted plants reserved for their leisure time.

The ship carried 800 passengers housed in two main decks and one top deck (first class). From what we saw most cabins had four berths, and all opened onto the deck. The passengers, including many family groups, were obviously enjoying the trip. Details of the route were written up on several large boards (alas, only in Chinese script) and light refreshments were available from small buffets.

Apart from the magnificent scenery, the greatest interest came at the stopping places. Here small crowds of people stood on the steps from the floating landing stages, to watch the loading and unloading of cargo, while passengers carrying anything from furniture and packing cases to shoulder poles and baskets of vegetables, crowded on to the boat. From time to time members of the crew could be seen meeting families and friends and exchanging packages. Obviously there were great advantages for all concerned when a crew member could make purchases in one of the big cities for the family 'back home'. From our top deck we had a splendid view of all these reunions and transactions: a panorama of the busy life along this special part of the great river, fraught with difficulty and danger in the past, now more or less tamed at last, its beauty and splendour available for the delight of not only the Chinese themselves, but for the fortunate travellers from other parts of the world who have been privileged to visit it. For unless the plans of the Chinese government can be changed, much of this wonderful area is doomed to disappear for ever beneath the waters of one of the largest man-made lakes in the world, in the Three Gorges Project.

The idea of a dam across the Yangtze in the Gorges area is not new. It was first suggested in 1919 by Sun Yat-Sen and investigations took place in the 1940s. In 1956 Mao Zedong, after his famous swim in the Yangtze wrote a poem in which he looked forward to the bridging of the Yangtze at Wuhan (opened in 1957) and the building of a dam in the gorges:

> Great plans are afoot:
> A bridge will fly to span the north and south,
> Turning a deep chasm into a thoroughfare;
> Walls of stone will stand upstream to the west
> To hold back Wushan's clouds and rain
> Till a smooth lake rises in the narrow gorges.
> The mountain goddess if she is still there
> Will marvel at a world so changed.[68]

His idea that man should strive to master Nature was in great contrast to the old Daoist doctrine of going along with Nature and where necessary 'bending to the wind'. The classical Chinese verse structures of his poems shows that he was still in some ways a traditionalist.

The aim of the project was fourfold: to control flooding, to aid navigation, to produce hydroelectric power, and to help in irrigation of drought areas. During the past 2000 years the river has caused 214 flood disasters, or one every six to ten

---

[68] Mao Tsetung, *Poems*, Beijing: Foreign Languages Press, 1976, p31.

years, those of 1870 (the worst for 800 years) 1931 and 1935 (more than one million drowned) and 1954 being particularly severe. In 1981 the flow of the river at Yichang was the highest for 30 years. In 1954 a serious disaster in the Jingjiang area was only averted by the fact that 300,000 people had been involved in flood diversion and dyke raising during the past two years.

At one time Dongting and Boyang acted as natural reservoirs, but silting and land reclamation reduced their capacity. Marco Polo on his return to Venice reported that the river was 16km wide in the Dongting area, but was not believed. The flatness of the land between the gorges and the sea is made clear by the fact that the town of Yichang is 40m above sea level, but 1540km from the sea, giving an approximate fall of 1m in 38km. From 1949 onwards there were constant efforts to improve the situation, by dyke-building, river-straightening, and the building of the large retention basin at Shasi. In the 1980s the great Gezhouba Dam was erected just above Yichang. However, the dream of a much larger project persisted, and following the great flood disaster of 1954, a report was commissioned, and published in 1958. After nearly 30 years in limbo, discussions began again. The chosen site was at Sandouping, rather more than 40km above Gezhouba. In 1985 a new report suggested further research before a final decision, so in June 1986 a new group was formed to undertake a complete re-study. Experts from Canada and the World Bank joined in and after two-and-a-half years issued a report in 14 parts, 9 of which were unanimously supported. Ten experts and advisers did not sign the remaining five reports, because they disagreed with the conclusions. The final report was issued in March 1989. In 1991 extensive floods in the middle reaches of the Yangtze caused losses amounting to more than the proposed cost of the dam, and in March 1992 the National People's Congress finally endorsed the scheme.

There are still dissentient voices both in China and abroad, but after so many years of discussion and thorough research it is understandable that the Government should wish to go ahead. The project will take about 18 years to complete, and well-wishers can only hope that problems still outstanding will be solved en route.

In 1993, the magazine *China Today*, which organises tours for its readers, offered one entitled 'Farewell to the Yangtze River's Three Gorges'.[69] Those who have had the privilege of making what is surely one of the finest river journeys in the world can feel only sorrow at the loss. The fortunate few able to make the farewell trip would have done well to prepare for it by reading as much as possible of the geology, history, legends and life of the great river. 'He who would bring back the wealth of the Indies must take the wealth of the Indies with him.'

[69] *China Today*, May 1993, p36.

5

DOWN THE LONG RIVER III

The Lake Basins, the Water Country, the Ancient Kingdom of Chu, and the Three Kingdoms

Archibald Little began his journey through the gorges at Yichang, where he stayed for a time in a fine Chinese house and recorded his surprise that the occupants were all in bed by 8pm. He describes several trips to the east and south of the city, accompanied by a coolie carrying a shoulder pole from which two baskets were suspended. One contained two double blankets and the other two loaves of brown bread, one tin of milk, one tin of Bass, and one tin of cocoa. He always refers to the cocoa as his 'Cadbury', and says it is 'indispensable' when travelling in winter among 'savourless nations'. On his trips he 'cooked' his 'Cadbury' himself, and drank it with a supper of mountain rice and bean curd. His bill at a local hotel, where he had supper, bed, and breakfast, makes interesting reading:

Supper (self and coolie) 4 bowls rice (10 copper cash each) with fixings of cabbage and bean curd (free)	40
Use of straw plaited mattress (2 at 10 each)	20
Breakfast (same as supper)	40
Supper and breakfast for my dog (Nigger)	20
Pair of straw sandals for coolie (old ones worn out)	12
Total in copper cash	132

Equivalent in English money at that time – 6 pence.[70]

---

[70]Archibald Little, *Through the Yang-Tse Gorges*, London: Sampson Low and Co, 1888, Chap 3.

A dramatic scenic change takes place as one emerges from the gorges at Yichang. The clanging of the stonecutters in the Xiling Gorge is silenced, and the pyramidal green hills on the river bank opposite the city look artificial and toy-like after the magnificent precipices of the gorges. The Changjiang now enters the area of Dongting Lake, merging with it during the high-water season, and threading its way through the mud flats at times of low water level.

The writer saw it in September 1979 as a wide calm sea, in which river and lake would have been indistinguishable, but for the well-marked navigation channel. Small craft sometimes become stranded on the mud as the water level falls, and remain there for months until it rises again.

This area is the main 'Rice Bowl' of China, consisting of the basins of Lakes Dongting and Boyang and the intensely cultivated Delta. Most of the region is double cropped, and in addition to vast quantities of rice, large amounts of wheat, beans, sweet potatoes, maize, oilseeds, and many varieties of fruit and vegetables are grown, as well as mulberry trees for silk worms, and tea on the hillslopes. Rice is a very labour-intensive crop with the preparation of seed beds and flooded fields and the transplanting and harvesting, still being carried out mainly by traditional methods, with the assistance of water buffalo. Several attempts have been made to perfect a mechanical rice transplanter, but without great success. Some small machinery has however reduced the burden of farm labour to a certain extent. Pumps worked by electricity or diesel oil have replaced the dragon's back water wheel and the treadle pump for lifting and distributing water. In particular, the small diesel-driven 8hp tractor has been a boon all over China. It is very versatile, and can be used in a stationary position for chopping, cutting, and grinding, as well as for work in the fields, and quite often as a substitute horse harnessed to small cartloads of produce or water containers. In fact its popularity became so great that songs were written about it. Here is one:

Four men carry our motor
To run it only one is needed
On the hillside or the plains
High or low our fields are watered.

Various forms of wheelbarrow, a Chinese invention, are still pushed, or pulled along the narrow raised paths between the flat fields. The bicycle is a useful substitute, and can often be seen fantastically loaded with carefully balanced baskets and sacks, leaving just enough room for the rider.

Leaving the Dongting area, the river enters the second great Lake Basin, that of Lake Boyang, China's largest fresh-water lake, measuring 170km from north to south, and 50 to 70km from east to west. During the summer the water surface covers an area of 2850km^2 falling to 500km^2 during the dry season. At that time the lake is divided into many smaller shallow ones interspersed with muddy land, marshes and small islets, ideal for water birds of many types, especially winter migrants. The area is less densely populated than that round Dongting, where economic development has polluted the water with industrial waste, pesticides, and chemical fertilizers. One hundred and fifty species of birds, including 81 on the protected list, have been seen on Lake Boyang, including swans, storks, mandarin ducks and most important, cranes. Local people have always hunted the wild birds, and between 1976 and 1981, thousands are known to have been shot. A visit of scientists in 1982 led to the banning of hunting, and the establishment of the Boyang Lake Migrant Birds Nature Reserve in 1983. This happened just in time before the discovery in January 1984 of 700 Siberian cranes wintering on the Lake. The species was thought to be on the verge of extinction, so the event caused great excitement among the expert ornithologists of the International Crane Foundation, and in China, where the crane has for centuries held a special place in legend, poetry and painting. It is mentioned in the ancient *Book of Songs* dated 800 to 600 BC. Recently its numbers had decreased dramatically in all its known breeding sites and venues, so there is now a great stimulus to research on its present whereabouts and migration routes.[71]

Beyond Boyang, the great river enters the true 'water country' of the Yangtze Delta, another exquisite man-made landscape, comparable in beauty to the Chengdu Plain of Sichuan. Here are three of China's most famous ancient cities, Nanjing, the 'Southern Capital', Hangzhou with its beautiful West Lake described by Marco Polo, and Suzhou, the 'Venice of the East' its waterways interspersed with some of the most beautiful gardens created by the mandarins, the élite members of the Chinese Civil Service, for their retirement. Finally, the premier Chinese port of Shanghai, with a population of 11 million, of which 5 million live in the main city. Now a huge industrial centre, Shanghai has become more cosmopolitan and sophisticated, and its inhabitants regard themselves as trend setters for the rest of China.

The rural landscape in the Delta is an object lesson in integrated farming. The villages are on higher ground, which is also used for mulberry trees and the ever useful bamboo. Mulberry leaves provide food for silkworms, and winter feed for sheep, kept as a sideline for wool and skins. The sheep manure and the silkworms' cocoons provide fertilizer for the trees and for the fish ponds, while the mud from the fish ponds is fertilizer for the rice fields. Grass along the banks between the rice fields provides summer food for sheep and water buffaloes, while the web of canals is used for transport and duck-farming. The general prosperity of the peasants is evident from the elegance of the houses, many of which now boast new brick extensions. Between Shanghai and Hangzhou many houses show, instead of the typical upturned gable ends, protruding curved beams on the main roof timber, the part we once called the roof-tree. This has a strange effect. Seen in silhouette against the sky it appears that slim boats with upturned prows and sterns have been laid along the rooftops.

---

[71]Tang Xiyang, *Living Treasures: An Odyssey Through China's Extraordinary Nature Reserves*, Bantam Books, 1987.

It is to be hoped that the interesting regional characteristics of Chinese houses will have been recorded before they disappear beneath the rising tide of utilitarian development.

The Lake Basins of the middle Yangtze and the Delta area were the site of a second 'cradle of Chinese civilization' following that of the Huanghe area. The ancient kingdom of Chu, which occupied most of the region, including much of present Hunan, developed a culture which lasted more than a 1000 years until 223 BC when it was overrun by the Qin army of Shihuangdi, the first emperor of unified China: as early as Shang times (15th–11th century BC) settlers from the north began to colonise the Yangtze area, and during the 13th century BC the Shang had hoped to incorporate Chu into their empire. However, they were overcome by the Zhou, and by the 11th century BC Chu had become a vassal state of Zhou. There was much unrest during the next few centuries, and by about 740 BC the ruler of Chu became a king in his own right, and his kingdom became increasingly powerful, as the many smaller states were absorbed into the 'big seven' kingdoms which succeeded the Zhou empire. Chu reached the zenith of its greatness by the 4th century BC. It is interesting to note that in the past when peoples have moved from bleak or severe environments to a richer more varied area, the stimulation has sometimes led after a time, to a flowering of civilization. The ancient Greeks were a possible example, coming as they probably did from the steppes north of the Black Sea to the light and beauty of the Aegean, where they developed one of the greatest of ancient cultures. Similarly the Aryans, entering the luxuriant forests of the Ganges valley, at first found the new surroundings strange and forbidding, but later, mixed with the indigenous people and adapted to the environment, they produced the rich treasure house of Sanskrit literature. Perhaps, in China, the movement to the Changjiang valley with its splendid scenery, and great variety of birds, trees, and flowers, stimulated the passionate response to Nature of the poets and painters of Chu, which nourished the Han dynasty and was to be fulfilled in later centuries of poetry and painting. A minister of state of the Chu court at the end of the 4th century wrote a poem which was to distinguish him as the 'father of Chinese poetry', or 'the first poet of China', and set a pattern and style which would be followed by generations down to the golden age of Chinese poetry in the Tang dynasty (618–906 AD). His name was Qu Yuan. Born about 340 BC in a former Chu capital (now Zigui), of noble descent, he became a statesman at the Chu court, where he attacked the current corruption, and was dismissed. He returned later, continued his reproaches, and was finally banished as a result of slander and intrigue by other courtiers. His most famous poem *Li Sao* (Encountering Sorrow) was written in protest at his unjust treatment. The last lines of the poem read:

> Enough! There are no true men in the state: no one understands me.
> Why should I cleave to the city of my birth?
> Since none is worthy to work with in making good government,
> I shall go and join Peng Xian[72] in the place where he abides.[73]

Qu Yuan has come down in popular folk-lore as the supreme example of the incorruptible statesman. It is said that on the 5th day of the 5th month in the year 278 BC he heard the news that the Qin army had entered the capital of Chu, whereupon he tied himself to a large stone and committed suicide by plunging into the Milou river. Legend says that as he was wandering dejected along the river bank, a fisherman called out to him 'Are you not Lord of the Three Wards? What has brought you to this pass?'

'Because all the world is muddy and I alone am clear' said Qu Yuan, 'and because all men are drunk and I alone am

---

[72]Peng Xian: a righteous minister at the court of a Shang king: he drowned himself when his advice was not taken.
[73]David Hawkes, *The Songs of the South*, (Penguin Classics), Harmondsworth: Penguin, 1985, p78.

sober, I have been sent into exile.' The fisherman replied that the wise man can move as the world moves, and Qu Yuan asked how he could submit his spotless purity to the dirt of others. The fisherman smiled and paddled off, singing:

> When the Cang-lang's waters are clear,
> I can wash my hat-strings[74] in them;
> When the Cang-lang's waters are muddy,
> I can wash my feet in them.[75,76]

He then vanished.

The life of Qu Yuan became a cult in Han times. By the 5th century AD the annual festival and sacrifice to the water dragons was changed to a celebration in his honour, and the famous Dragon Boat Races, held on the 5th day of the 5th lunar month are still performed in his memory. In many places in Central and South China it is one of the most colourful festivals of the year, with the race of the Dragon Boats as the exciting and noisy climax, the shouting of the crowds mingling with the din of gongs, drums and firecrackers. Boats can be as much as 27m long, with 40 pairs of 'paddlers'. Large dragon heads decorate the prows, the jaws opening and shutting as the boat skims across the water.

It is said that people used to row out on the river every year on that special day and throw rice into the water as 'food' for Qu Yuan's spirit. Later the rice was wrapped in bamboo leaves to protect it from fish, and later still other ingredients were added to become the famous 'zongzi', which are always eaten at the time of this festival. In ancient times these contained glutinous rice, chopped dates, persimmons, gingko, and red beans stuffed into hollow bamboo and placed in the river to placate demons or please dragons.[77] In 1987 the writer was staying with a Chinese family in north-west Malaysia. Like all exiles they were keen to celebrate traditional festivals. After an expedition

[74]Hat strings were a badge of rank.
[75]Meaning: that one should adapt to circumstances.
[76]Ibid. p207.
[77]*China Reconstructs*, June 1987, p8.

to a Chinese shop in the nearest town, Ipoh, to purchase the necessary ingredients (expense no problem!), the women sat at a round table in the kitchen preparing the *zongzi*, correct to the last detail, including the special leaves used as wrapping. After boiling they were hung outside under a roof to dry. They were duly consumed with great pleasure on the Special Day.

There is little doubt that these celebrations originated long before Qu Yuan's time but 'time changes the tune', and successive generations adapt old festivals to new heroes. Qu Yuan's reputation was enhanced by the admiration accorded him by the literati, whose idea of honour he fulfilled by speaking out fearlessly against corruption in high places. During the war with Japan in 1937–1945 Qu Yuan was publicized as a great patriotic poet, and this idea was carried on into Communist times when a book for high school students praising his work was published in 1957.

Poetically he is unassailable. He initiated a completely new type of poetry, different from the old 'songs' which were spoken or sung as featured in the *Shi Jing*. The poetry of the *Chu Ci* (*Songs of the South*) by contrast is personal and literary. It incorporates many elements of shamanism, once thought to have originated among the aboriginal tribes of central China, but now recognized as the original religion of north China as well. The 'spirit journey' of the shamans is used in Qu Yuan's great poem as an allegory of the alternatives open to him after his dismissal and exile. The famous Tang poet Li Bai was often attracted by the idea of 'spirit' or 'dream' travelling, and shamanistic influences appear in Chinese painting as in 'Dreaming of Immortality in a Thatched Cottage' probably by Zhou Chen (flourished about 1500–1535), a horizontal scroll showing a scholar asleep in his country retreat on the right hand side of the picture, while away on the left above misty mountains, he is seen making a 'spirit journey' in the sky, to the land of the immortals.[78] The

---

[78]James Cahill, *Chinese Painting*, (Treasures of Asia Series), London: A. Skira Macmillan, 1977, p138–139.

Chu Ci is an anthology of poems by Qu Yuan and his school, compiled in the 2nd century AD during the Han dynasty. The arguments as to which poems are by the master and which by his 'followers' can never be settled finally, though there is no doubt about the authorship of the great first poem, *Li Sao*. It reveals the depth of learning of Qu Yuan, both of shamanistic and other legends, and the plants used in ancient herbal medicine. Indeed it has been called the most 'botanical' poem ever written. Other poems in the collection generally attributed to the master are *The Great Summons* (Da Shou), *In Praise of the Orange Tree* (Ju Song) and *Heavenly Questions* (Tian Wen).

The Great Summons refers to a shamanistic ritual to bring back to a body a soul which has wandered off in a dream or in approaching death: persuasion and threats were used. In this example, it is the soul of a dying king which is being addressed. The poem was probably written by a follower of Qu Yuan, but definitely in his style, and it is interesting for the information it gives on the culture and lifestyle of Chu. After threatening the soul with the dangers of North, South, East, and West, persuasion takes over:

Where thirty cubits high at harvest-time
The corn is stacked;
Where pies are cooked of millet and water-grain,
Guests watch the steaming bowls
And sniff the pungency of peppered herbs.
The cunning cook adds slices of bird-flesh,
Pigeon and yellow-heron and black-crane.
They taste the badger-stew.
O soul come back to feed on foods you love!

A summer-house with spacious rooms
And a high hall with beams stained red;
A little closet in the southern wing
Reached by a private stair.
And round the house a covered way should run
Where horses might be trained.

And sometimes riding, sometimes going afoot
You shall explore, O Soul, the parks of spring;
Your jewelled axles gleaming in the sun
And yoke inlaid with gold;
Or amid orchises and sandal-trees
Shall walk in the dark woods.
O Soul come back and live for these delights!

Other verses refer to wines, to music on the lute, harp, flute, and bells, and to singers and dancing girls. At the end the soul is summoned to come back and continue the work of good government:

Fields, villages and lanes
Shall throng with happy men;
Good rule protect the people and make known
The King's benevolence to all the land;
Stern discipline prepare
Their natures for the soft caress of Art.
O Soul come back to where the good are praised![79]

In Europe we usually regard the orange tree as a product of the Mediterranean, forgetting that it originally came via the great trade routes, from Central and South China, particularly the Yangtze valley. The poem *In Praise of the Orange Tree* is thought by some to be an early work of Qu Yuan himself:

Fairest of all God's trees, the orange tree came
  and settled here,
Commanded by him not to move, but only grow
  in the South Country,
Deep-rooted, firm and hard to shift: showing in
  this its singleness of purpose;

---

[79]Arthur Waley, *Chinese Poems*, London: George Allen and Unwin, 1961, p34–37.

Its leaves of green and pure white blossoms
delight the eye of the beholder,
And the thick branches and spines so sharp,
and the fine round fruits
Green ones with yellow intermingling to
make a pattern of gleaming brightness
Pure white beneath the rich-hued surface: a
parable of virtuous living;
Its lusty growth to gardener's art respondent:
producing beauty without blemish.

In *Heavenly Questions* it appears that Qu Yuan was adapting an ancient text, which he rearranged: archaic riddles with shamanistic associations are mixed with philosophical questions: here are a few examples:

Who passed down the story of the far-off,
ancient beginning of things? How can we be
sure what it was like before the sky above
and the earth below had taken shape?...

What manner of things are the darkness and light?...

Whose compass measured out the ninefold heavens?...

How does heaven co-ordinate its motions?...
How do the sun and the moon hold to their courses and
the fixed stars keep their places?

When High God in heaven confers His mandate,
how does He give notice of it? When He
has bestowed dominion over the world on one,
why does he take it away and give it to another?[80]

The frustration and despair expressed by Qu Yuan in *Li Sao* was echoed by many poets who followed him but did not

[80]David Hawkes, *The Songs of the South*, (Penguin Classics), Harmondsworth: Penguin, 1985, pp178, 127 and 133.

achieve his excellence. The more successful court poets adapted the shamanistic elements to the necessarily more cheerful style required of them. The achievements of Chu civilization which survived the Qin conquest, offered a rich heritage to the succeeding Han dynasty, not only in literature, but in the arts and crafts of wood carving, metal and lacquer work, silk manufacture, music and dance. Recent excavations have unearthed thousands of tombs in the former area of Chu, and the richness and variety of their contents has led to the setting up of a Chu Culture Research Society in China. An outstanding example was the opening-up of the tomb of the 'Old Lady of Mawangdui' near Changsha. She was a lady of rank in Han times and her tomb contained musical instruments, household goods, and many fine items of lacquer ware, as well as silk clothing, and a silk banner on which were depicted items of mythology relating to shamanistic elements in *Songs of the South*.

Echoes of Qu Yuan continue to reverberate down the centuries. In the autumn of 1979 the writer visited the great conurbation of Wuhan: originally there were three cities: Hankou and Hanyang on the north bank, and Wuchang on the south. Now Wuhan has become a very important industrial centre and river port, and is the site of the first road and rail bridge across the Changjiang. Wuchang is the administrative centre, and houses the local university. Nearby is the beautiful East Lake surrounded by a fine park. Sometimes a combination of weather, surroundings, history and legend, can combine to produce a unique experience. The lake-side path was bordered by pine trees and oleanders, and redolent with the enchanting scent of osmanthus blossom. We turned a corner, and came face to face with a modern pure white statue of Qu Yuan. Tall and dignified, dressed in the flowing robes of ancient China, he was gazing eastwards over his beloved land of Chu. The head and face of the statue resembled those of the terracotta warriors of Xi'an; the short beard, the strong features, the hair twisted in an elaborate top-knot. We were further seduced by the sound of music and came upon a group of young men beside the lake playing ancient instruments. We were told that they did this regularly during their lunch break. We joined the small crowd under the trees to listen. At that moment we noticed a small fishing boat approaching. An old man, holding a steering pole, stood upright in the boat, his wrinkled face, with its small straggly beard, surmounted by a large hat; a perfect picture of old China. Silently he brought the boat to the bank, and sat down to listen to the music. Qu Yuan, and now the Fisherman! A moment of magic by the East Lake.

In a recent programme in Channel 4's series *Orientations* a Chinese girl sang from the poem *Questions to Heaven*, accompanied by modern pop-style music to a background of changing skies and landscapes.

It has been said that the Chinese are 'weighed down by history' and that 'the trouble with Chinese history is that there is so much of it.' Looking at the complex drama of events from 221 BC until 1998, a span of over 2000 years, a rough pattern can be discerned: periods of stability during the great dynasties such as the Han, Tang, Ming and Qing, often lasting for 300 years or more, during which great progress was made in civilization: these interspersed with episodes of disunity and chaos, sometimes known as 'panics'. In spite of these the essential continuity never broke completely, giving China the record of the longest continuous civilization the world has known.

Such a period of confusion and disunity occurred during the closing years of the great Han dynasty, which ended in 220 AD, after which complete unity was not to be achieved again until 400 years later, with the establishment of the Tang. The first 45 years from 220 until 265 became known as the time of the Three Kingdoms (Wei, Shu, and Wu), immortalized in the famous book *The Romance of the Three Kingdoms*. In 184 AD the Han dynasty, which had become weak and corrupt, was undermined in a rebellion instigated by a secret society known as the 'Yellow Turbans'. The imperial chancellor, Cao Cao, had been plotting to overthrow the Emperor and by 210 AD he and his family were dominating most of north China, and were already setting their sights on the centre and south. Allied against them were Liu Bei, a relation of the imperial family, determined to restore the Han dynasty and Sun Quan, from the lower Changjiang area.

In 208 AD a decisive battle took place in the central Changjiang area, known as the 'Battle of the Red Cliff', which put an end to Cao Cao's dreams of a southern empire. Modern tourists approaching Wuhan by river from the west, are shown the site. The writer remembers a complete exit from the dining saloon in the middle of lunch as everyone rushed out to view the spot. Cao Cao was encamped with a fleet of ships, and it was said a million men (it was probably nearer 200,000!) on the North bank of the Changjiang, facing the army (about 10,000 men) and ships of the 'Southland', and its allies, on the opposite side. The battle was remarkable for the use of trickery combined with Daoist magic on the part of the 'Southland'. Spies and defectors passed back and forth constantly between the rival forces, probing secrets and spreading rumours. Three dramatic episodes took place: the 'borrowing of arrows': the summoning of the unseasonal East wind: the final attack by the fireships.

The Southland had run short of arrows, but managed to acquire a large supply by feigning an attack, under the cover of a thick fog. Twenty boats, on which bales of straw covered with black cloth had been arranged to look like soldiers lined up on the ships took part. Cao Cao mistook this for an ambush, and ordered his bowmen to fire at random. A storm of arrows penetrated the straw 'soldiers' and soon the Southland ships vanished into the fog with their booty.

The Southland leaders then consulted, and decided on a plan to set fire to Cao Cao's fleet. However, to succeed in this, an easterly or south easterly wind, almost unknown at this time of the year, would be needed. One of the leaders then revealed that he had once been given, (presumably by a Daoist priest), divine texts which explained how to call forth winds and rain. Instructions for building a tower, to be called the 'Platform of the Seven Stars' were included, with exact measurements, and details of the necessary ritual. The tower was soon built of earth in three 1m tiers, each adorned with flags and symbols representing important constellations, lines from the *Book of*

Changes (*Yi Jing*), and the banner of the Seven fixed Stars. At the approved time, the 20th day of the 11th lunar month, the leader concerned put on the vestments of a Daoist priest, lit the incense, poured water into a vessel and performed the required silent incantations. For hours no wind appeared, and he had reached the point where his life was threatened as a punishment for deception, when suddenly they heard the distant murmur of the rising wind and soon a strong gale was blowing from the south-east. The fireships were already prepared.

Cao Cao had been told by a defector-turned-traitor that a fleet of grain ships was to be expected, but these were no grain ships. They were loaded with stacks of reeds, drenched with fish-oil, and spread with a compound of sulphur and saltpetre, all covered with black cloth. Too late Cao Cao realized he had been tricked, as the ships were torched, and blazing with flame and smoke they sped 'like arrows in flight' into the chained and crowded fleet, demolishing it completely. Thus ended the great battle. Cao Cao and the remnants of his army escaped to the north.[81,82]

Within the next 15 years Liu Bei took control in Sichuan, founded the empire of Shu Han and declared himself 'emperor': Cao Cao died in 220, the year when the Han dynasty finally ended and his son became 'emperor' of Wei, and Sun Quan established himself in Nanjing and declared himself emperor of Wu in 222 AD. Thus began the period known as the Three Kingdoms, which was to last until 265 AD, ushering in a brief period of peace during which agriculture flourished. In Shù the ancient irrigation system, Dujiangyan, was repaired and maintained, and silk weaving developed to the stage where the brocades of Chengdu became famous throughout China. In the kingdom of Wu shipbuilding became important, leading to increased links between the mainland and Taiwan.

---

[81] *Three Kingdoms: China's Epic Drama*, trans. and ed. Moss Roberts, New York: Pantheon Books, 1976.
[82] Jacques Gernet, *A History of Chinese Civilization*, trans. R. Foster, Cambridge: CUP, 1982, pp176, 694–695.

6

UPHEAVAL IN THE COUNTRYSIDE 1949 TO 1993

Perhaps this is a suitable moment at which to take a look at the immense upheavals of the last 40 years, which have brought about stupendous changes in the lives of China's 800 million peasants. Many people saw the coming of Communism in the 1950s as an answer to thousands of years of oppression of the peasants by cruel landlords. From time to time peasant uprisings had had partial success in dethroning Emperors, or mitigating for a time some of the worst features of the system. In the revolution of 1911, one of the watchwords of Sun Yat-Sen had been 'The Land to the Tiller', but this had not come about, and the 1920s was a chaotic time of war-lords and private armies, with many villages putting out containers of 'peace rice' to keep away marauding soldiers. The new Red Army of the Communists with its strict discipline and good behaviour towards the peasants came as a revelation. It seemed that a new age was dawning: the tyranny of the landlords had vanished: the land now belonged to the peasants. In Communist-held areas land reform had begun several years before the final triumph of 1949. Confiscated land was redistributed to individual peasants who became private owners. However, it soon became clear that many could not cope on their own, and Mutual Aid Teams were developed, followed by the Agricultural Producers' Co-operatives where the ownership of tools and machines was collectivized though the land still remained private property. The move towards complete collectivization gathered pace and by 1957 the stage was set for the creation of the People's Communes.

Agriculture was now organized on a completely collective basis, with a chain of authority and discussion running down from the Commune (average population 50 to 60 thousand) through the Brigades to the Teams, which were roughly equivalent to a village. Discussions and decisions on the use of the land, variety of crops, and work programmes, took place at each of the three levels. Payment was by a system of work points, which determined the share of produce and/or cash due to each individual or family. In an excess of enthusiasm for the collective, normal family life was thought to be unnecessary; to free the women for communal work, young children were looked after in nurseries and kindergartens, and meals were served in mass dining halls. These arrangements were short-lived, as the strong tradition of the Chinese family soon reasserted itself and life became more normal. There is no doubt, however, that there were considerable gains for some peasants. Collective structures meant that land-use became more efficient, the all-important management of water was taken care of, and the more prosperous communes were able to raise living standards considerably by investing in clinics and hospitals, housing and schools, and initiating small rural industries. The 'barefoot doctors' did much to spread hygiene and health-care in rural areas, and were responsible for an immunization programme covering millions of children.

In the later half of the 1950s it appeared to many that the bad old days had gone for ever: the frequent famines; the selling of girl children into what in some cases was little short of slavery; female infanticide resulting from desperate poverty; widespread disease; all these seemed relegated to the past. Mao Zedong announced proudly that 'The Chinese people have stood up,' and the rest of the world looked on with admiration or trepidation, depending on political alignment. Some thought that the Chinese had found a solution which could be applied in many parts of the Third World. In 1974 an American wrote 'The Chinese have tapped a major source of ego incentive in the context of participatory management ... perception that everyone is doing their fair share of hard work, ... and people in authority are not usurping privileges.'[83] Opinion in the West was greatly influenced by reports from a small number of sympathisers of the regime who lived in China for a time and wrote of their experiences. An American journalist, Edgar Snow, went to China in the 1930s, and lived there for seven years. He lectured at Yenching University in Beijing and came to know personally many future Communist leaders including Mao Zedong and Zhou Enlai. He wrote two books which have become classics, *Red Star over China*, and *The Other Side of the River*. He died in 1972, leaving a third book *China's Long Revolution* unfinished, but it was completed by a friend and later published.

Another American, William Hinton, and a Swede, Jan Myrdal, lived for a time in villages in north China, and wrote detailed accounts of rural life under Communism. Both revisited the area some years later and recorded the changes which had taken place. Rewi Alley, a New Zealander, made his home in China for over 30 years, and was a keen supporter of Communist policies, as was Felix Greene, an American who travelled extensively in China and wrote *The Wall has Two Sides*, a panegyric of the new China.

Some of the propaganda in China itself seemed to idealists in the West to have near-Christian connotations. A good example was called the 'Three Old Stories' which all Communists were encouraged to read. The first was the story of a Canadian doctor, Norman Bethune, who died serving the soldiers of the Red Army. His 'utter devotion to others' was extolled as an example to every Communist, particularly as he came from another country, thus showing a spirit of true internationalism. The second, 'Serve the People' was a speech by Mao praising an ordinary soldier who died a 'worthy death', and the third was an ancient Chinese legend 'The Foolish Old Man who

---

[83]S. Andors, 'Hobbes and Weber vs. Marx and Mao: the Political Economy of Decentralization in China', *Bulletin of Concerned Asian Scholars*, 1974, Vol 6 No 3, p19–34.

Removed the Mountains'. An old man of 90 lived opposite two mountains which blocked the way for travellers, so he called his family together and suggested that they should cut a way through. All agreed except his wife, who taunted him with his lack of strength. However, his two sons were ready to try, and off they went with pickaxes and baskets. The small son of a nearby widow joined them. The Wise Old Man of the River Bend ridiculed them, but the Foolish Old Man replied that while nothing would be added to the mountains, his sons and grandsons and their descendants would go on cutting away for centuries, until at last the mountains would be removed. The Emperor of Heaven was moved by the Old Man's faith, and sent spirits to remove the mountains, since when the area has been an unbroken plain. Mao said the mountains were the two evils which held back China, feudalism and imperialism, and that they would be defeated by the Chinese 'masses', the people, 'digging together'. In 1976, from the train on the Guangzhou-Beijing railway, the writer saw an enormous line of Chinese characters along the hillside to the West, and the guide said that they read 'Remember the Foolish Old Man'. Seven years later, on repeating the journey, there was no sign of the inscription!

In November 1976, just after the death of Mao, copies of the 'Little Red Book', the 'Thoughts of Mao' were still being presented to visitors to China. It was small and flexible and had the look and feel of a prayer book: the frontispiece was a portrait of Mao covered with tissue paper, and the Thoughts were printed under subject headings. The people were persuaded to study them carefully during work-breaks in field and factory, and at special sessions, where extracts were read and discussed in the manner of Bible-study meetings in Christian churches.

There is no doubt that a great deal of enthusiasm and genuine idealism went into the first ten years of the Communist regime. Professor Tuzo Wilson, the distinguished Canadian geophysicist, and President of the International Union of Geodesy and Geophysics, visited China in 1958 as the guest of Academia Sinica. His visit was concerned with science, and he was impressed beyond his expectations by the progress and the tremendous enthusiasm for education which he found. His journeys around the country convinced him that this was certainly, in his own words, 'no slave state'.

The development from individual peasant farms to the People's Communes of 1958 had been rushed through at an accelerating pace, and from then on a series of events occurred which slowed down the progress towards real Communism which had been the dream of the 1949 Revolution. What went wrong? Some observers, 'old China hands' like a former East Asia correspondent, suggested that the Chinese, with their traditional love of 'order under Heaven' resented being continually hectored and stirred up. From 1958 until 1976 the pot was certainly stirred again and again. Swings to the Right and the Left became a constant feature of the government in Beijing. The establishment of the Communes was followed by the Great Leap Forward and the fiasco of the 'backyard' steel making. The early 1960s were a time of exceptionally bad weather, with poor harvests leading to famine in some areas. Some of the stricter regulations were slightly reduced, but soon the swing to the Left set in which was to lead to the excesses of the Cultural Revolution. Revolutionary committees were established in every school, hospital, factory, and commune. They were there as watchdogs, to see that the political 'line' was correctly followed. The fear that any concessions to individual effort might encourage creeping capitalism led to the closing of thousands of rural markets, resulting in shortages of fruit and vegetables in towns and cities: certain products were forbidden on private plots: mulberry trees and tea gardens were destroyed in order to achieve the grain target. Peasants were told to 'take grain as the key link' and became afraid to diversify lest they be accused of 'taking the capitalist road'. The aim of socialism was not to enrich the workers, but to rid the world of exploitation of man by man, and eliminate the 'three great contests'. These were town versus country, industry versus agriculture and physical versus mental work. To achieve this millions of young people from the cities were sent down to the countryside to 'learn from the peasants', as were many intellectuals from universities and research institutes, with dire consequences for some of the valuable work which had been going on. The ancient peasant distrust of the intellectual élite often proved too strong for the new schemes, and led to much frustration and misunderstanding, while the movement against 'old things', leading to the loss of country fairs, and traditional forms of entertainment such as the various regional types of Chinese opera, reduced the quality of life for many people. By about 1964 Mao had become convinced that revolutionary enthusiasm was flagging, and that a new stimulus was needed, not from the Party officials but from a mass movement. Hence his famous poster 'Bombard the Headquarters', meaning the Party bosses. Schools and colleges were closed for six months, to enable young people to travel round the country, which they did in their thousands, travelling free on the railways. The Red Guards, consisting mainly of middle school teenagers, and some university students, committed many excesses in their rebellion against professional people, and set out to destroy all 'relics' of the past. Factions developed among them but from time to time they united in great rallies where hysterical adulation of Chairman Mao was a prominent feature.

As Mao's powers declined with increasing age, the 'Gang of Four', led by his wife Jiang Qing, took over more control of affairs, and Leftism held sway. Then in the fateful Year of the Dragon, 1976, everything came to a head. Zhou Enlai died in April, July saw the terrible Tangshan earthquake, and on October 9th Mao Zedong died. Three days earlier the Gang of Four had been arrested, to universal rejoicing. The writer visited China a month later, and was told that all the wine shops sold out as news of the arrest spread. The death of Mao left an enormous gap, and many people were uneasy about the future. Hua Guofeng, who succeeded Mao, was a rather colourless figure. Deng Xiaoping, who had been a close supporter of Mao in the early days, but started to disagree with him after the fiasco of the Great Leap Forward, had been disgraced as a 'rightist' in 1966, but returned to power in 1973, was disgraced again early in 1976, only to be reinstated once more in 1977. Hua Guofeng survived until 1981 as nominal head of the country, but in December 1978 Deng and his supporters proposed three fundamental reforms to stimulate output: the use of material incentives: market forces to be allowed to influence the price of goods: private ownership to be recognized as useful in a socialist economy. The policy of the Four Modernizations took over; they were to take place in agriculture, industry, science and technology, and defence. This was soon followed by the development of the Responsibility System, which became universal in 1983.

Thus the last ten years have seen yet another transformation of life in China, as the communes have disappeared, the farms are run by peasant families, and it is OK to get rich. Many peasants are leaving the land, hoping to find a well paid job and a better life in the cities. It has been estimated that 80 million peasants have left the land recently and are sleeping 'rough', often in railway stations. Some have been sent back to the countryside. History never quite repeats itself, but some of the problems of the 1950s are reappearing. Today the poorer peasant taking responsibility for a small piece of land, can still find himself unable to cope. In the 1950s Mutual Aid Teams developed. Now 'service centres' where peasants can get advice on farming, or even hire tools, are being set up. With 'every family for itself' it is proving difficult to organize the all important water management, so vital for irrigation and flood prevention. There is evidence that work formerly undertaken by Brigades and Communes has been neglected under the Responsibility System. At first there was an increase in output, and by 1985 the compulsory grain quotas were stopped in favour of government/peasant contracts for grain and cotton and other vital products. However, grain has never been a money-making crop, and free of the quota, many peasants turned to cash crops such as fruit, or even potted plants, or medicinal herbs, particularly those recommended as aphrodisiacs. The grain harvest has still not equalled that of 1984, and while some peasants, particularly those who had several sons before the 'one-child' policy was launched, and were thus able to take on larger areas of land, have become 'ten thousand yuan households', others have had to give up their land, and either go to work for richer peasants or swell the crowds seeking jobs in the cities, a Third World phenomenon never allowed under Communism, where permission was needed to move from country to city.

The success in feeding a quarter of the world's population even basically from only 7 per cent of its arable land has been a remarkable achievement. By dint of hard work and strict social control the Chinese managed to increase grain production in line with a huge growth in population, from 568 million in 1952 to 982 million in 1980. Despite the hiccup of the early sixties, by 1976 the overall picture was one of complete transformation from the China of the 1940s, but the next step was fraught with difficulty: the peasants were faced with almost endless hard work for the sake of future generations, not for themselves; higher standards were impossible without much more development of the infrastructure and of industry: the goal was for ever disappearing over the horizon. Somehow the government must find a way to bring the peasants nearer to the level of city-dwellers. The Responsibility System has had some success, but a price is already being paid for the comparatively few who have achieved a high standard of living. With the new encouragement to make money have come some of the unacceptable features of Western capitalism: the pursuit of wealth at almost any cost: a loss of community feeling and responsibility: unemployment: the reintroduction of drug-trafficking and prostitution: an increase in family break-up: the pollution of the environment. The Communists held that collective poverty was preferable to individual production: in 1976 a young Maoist told the author that she was prepared to wait for a silk garment until silk became available for everyone. Many peasants came to resent collective methods, and the fact that lazy workers were just as well off as those who made great efforts for no extra reward. They felt that their legitimate expectations were held down. In the words of a speech in 1979 by Chen Yun, a colleague of Deng, and a critic later of

Deng's reforms, 'They want to be reapers of the harvest, not offerings to adorn a tomb.'[84]

Sinophiles and Sinophobes alike watch anxiously as China struggles into the 21st century. With a population similar to that of USA, former USSR, and Europe put together, she faces enormous problems in trying to raise the standard of living of her people, and take her place among the industrial giants of the world. Her present policy is in direct contrast to that of the former USSR, where political reform has been considered to be the key to economic change. In China economic development is the priority. Time enough to consider democracy when prosperity has been obtained! Regional differences have always posed problems. During the Communist era there was much agonizing over the differing prosperity of the communes in the difficult north where it was a struggle to reap one good harvest, to the more generous centre and south, where two or three could be achieved.

[84]John Gittings, *China Changes Face*, Oxford: OUP, 1989, p108.

7

THE COSMIC LANDSCAPE I

Emperors and the Environment During the Great Dynasties

To the ancient Chinese the natural world was orderly, alive, and organic. The mountains were the bones of the earth, the rivers the arteries, the clouds and mists, the breath. Man was seen as an integral part of Nature and in Zhou times (1122 to 221 BC) elaborate rituals were devised to make contact with the spirit(s) behind the natural world. Imagination was as 'real' as reality, and in 'dream' or 'spirit' journeys (see p 88) the soul was thought to leave the body temporarily. Various methods were used to induce trances, and many attempts were made to find an elixir which would confer immortality, or at least prolong life for 200 to 500 years. The first Emperor, Shihuangdi, was obsessed with this, and sent emissaries all over the Empire to search for magicians with suitable recipes: all manner of drinks were concocted, some even containing mercury, which of course proved fatal!

These early magical beliefs, which can be found among many primitive people, in China became incorporated in the system known as Daoism. Its founder, Laozi, a near contemporary of Confucius (551–479 BC) is a half-legendary figure, and may well represent more than one man. His classic book, the *Daodejing*, may be a compilation of a number of writings put together about the third or fourth century BC. In contrast to the Confucian conception of man as a moral being responsible for his actions, the Daoists regarded him as no more important than any other object in the natural world, to which he must adapt himself in every way, 'bending with the wind' rather than exerting himself to try to influence the natural order of things. The Dao, which means the 'way' is the fundamental principle behind the Universe, nameless, unknowable, non-personal, and amoral. 'Tuning in' to it could be achieved, not by intellectual activity but by a type of mystical experience. Thus the roots of Daoism reach back into magical beliefs, and the shamanism which was probably the universal ancient religion of China.

Here is a description of Dao from the *Daodejing*:

> There is a thing confusedly formed,
> Born before heaven and earth
> Silent and void
> It stands alone and does not change,
> Goes round and does not weary.
> It is capable of being the mother of the world.
>
> I know not its name,
> So I style it 'the way'.
> . . .
> Man models himself on earth,
> Earth on heaven,
> Heaven on the way,
> And the way on that which is naturally so.[85]

Zhuangzi, an important early Daoist was, unlike Laozi, a real historical figure, and left a book which was named after him. He once told of dreaming that he was a butterfly, and when he awoke, he found it difficult to decide whether he was Zhuangzi dreaming that he was a butterfly, or a butterfly dreaming that he was Zhuangzi. A common subject in Chinese poetry is that of going to visit a Daoist hermit and being

[85]Lao Tzu, *Tao te Ching*, trans. D.C. Lau, Book One, XXV, (Penguin Classics), Harmondsworth: Penguin, 1968, p82.

unable to find him. A little poem by Jia Dao (777–841) reads:

Under a pine
I asked his pupil
Who said 'Master's
Gone gathering balm
Only somewhere
About the mountain:
The clouds so thick
That I don't know where'

Li Bai wrote on the same theme, describing the natural background in a way which links it to his love of 'spirit journeys': On visiting a Daoist master in the Tai Tian Mountains and not finding him.

Where the dogs bark by roaring waters,
Whose spray darkens the petals' colours,
Deep in the woods deer at times are seen;

The valley noon: one can hear no bell,
But wild bamboos cut across bright clouds,
Flying cascades hang from jasper peaks;

No one here knows which way you have gone:
Two, now three pines
I have lent against.[86]

The same atmosphere can be felt in Qu Yuan's encounter with the Fisherman (see p 86) and with the eccentric chanting Daoist with 'hempen sandals' and 'tattered clothes' in chapter I of the *Story of the Stone* the 18th century novel by Cao Xueqin.[87]

The rival systems of Confucianism and Daoism ebb and flow

---

[86]Arthur Cooper, *Li Po and Tu Fu*, (Penguin Classics), Harmondsworth: Penguin, 1973, p105–106.
[87]Cao Xueqin, *The Story of the Stone*, Vol I, trans. David Hawkes, (Penguin Classics), Harmondsworth: Penguin, 1973, p63–65.

throughout Chinese history, orthodoxy and formalism alternating with magic and imagination in the attitudes of the educated élite. These swings of the pendulum, combined with the fundamental common sense and practicality of the Chinese people, and the down-to-earth scepticism of most of the literati, probably prevented extreme excesses in either direction. Buddhism blended with many aspects of Daoism during the early Tang dynasty, bringing about an increased sensitivity to Nature: the fairies of Daoism merged with the Buddhist apsaras, and the bodhisattva Avalokitesvara changed sex and became Guanyin the Chinese goddess of mercy. By the 9th century, however, Confucian reaction had set in: monasteries were closed, and monks and nuns turned out into the world. Large numbers fled to Japan, and Buddhism in China suffered a blow from which it never fully recovered, although it has continued to exist there until the present time, and survived the anti-religious years of Communism.

The Chinese word for landscape, *shanshui* means 'mountains and water'. In the typical landscape of China Proper, mountains spring suddenly from wide alluvial plains, lacking the foothills and rolling country of other parts of the world. It is easy to see why in the earliest times, all mountains were regarded as sacred, the homes of deities and spirits, who required sacrifice and ritual. At one time the Han Emperors made an annual ascent of Mount Tai to perform the rites necessary to ensure a good harvest. Mount Tai is in Shandong province in north China, and is the most famous of the five, formerly nine, of the sacred mountains. It is 1524m high, and has a total of 7200 steps giving access to the summit for pilgrims. From the top, weather permitting, it is possible to see sunrise over the East China Sea, and sunset on the Huanghe. The famous Five Pines Pavilion marks the spot where the first emperor found shelter from a severe storm in 219 BC.

The other four sacred mountains were often Daoist monastic sites, later taken over by Buddhists, or in some cases, like Mount Heng in Hunan, remaining sacred to both. Mount Song in Henan has the oldest observatory in China, built in 1276 AD, and a fifteen-storey pagoda 1400 years old, as well as numerous temples. It is the birthplace of the Chan sect of Buddhism in China in about 495 AD, which later became very important in Japan as Zen. The remaining two sacred mountains are Mount Hua (2160m above sea-level) in eastern Shaanxi, the highest and most difficult to climb of the five, and a second Mount Heng, in north-east Shanxi, which has a famous Hanging Monastery, built along the side of a cliff.

It is interesting to note the changing attitude to mountains over the centuries in different cultures. At first they were often regarded with religious awe, tinged with fear. In China an anonymous poet of the early Han dynasty wrote of his distaste of mountains:

> Wildly uneven
> The bends of the mountain:
> The heart stands still
> With awe aghast.
> Broken and wild,
> Chilling the heart.
> In the deep woods tangle
> Tigers and leopards spring,
> Towering and rugged,
> The craggy rocks, frowning
> Crooked and interlocked
> The woods' gnarled trees.
>
> Oh prince, return. In the mountains
> You cannot stay long.

During the period of disunion which followed the break up of the Han dynasty in 210 AD there was a general reaction against the orthodoxy of the time and many scholars moved to the centre and south of China. By the fourth century AD the movement had grown to the point where the change to a kinder environment had produced a change in attitudes, and an aesthetic appreciation of the beauty of mountains was appearing. This preceded a similar change in Europe by well over a thousand years. In the early 5th century AD both landscape poetry and painting began to appear in the south and centre of China expressing the close harmony between man and Nature characteristic of Daoist influence. The poet Xie Lingyun lived at that time, and is said to have exemplified the trend. He was a Daoist who became a convert to Buddhism and joined a monastery. His particular delight was to walk in the mountains and he is credited with inventing special footwear resembling crampons.

His love of mountains is shown in the following poem:

At dawn with staff in hand I climbed the crags,
At dusk I made my camp among the mountains.
Only a few peaks rise as high as this house,
Facing the crags, it overlooks winding streams.
In front of its gates a vast forest stretches,
While boulders lie around its very steps.
Hemmed in by mountains, there seems no way out,
The track gets lost among the thick bamboos.
My visitors can never find their way,
And when they leave, forget the path they took.
The raging torrents rush on through the dusk,
The monkeys clamour shrilly through the night.
Deep in meditation, how can I part from Truth?
I cherish the Way and never will swerve from it.
My heart is one with the trees of late autumn,
My eyes delight in the buds of early spring,
I dwell with my constant companion and wait for my end,
Content to find peace through accepting the flux of things.
I only regret that there is no kindred soul,
To climb with me this ladder to the clouds in the blue.[88]

The Tang poet Li Bai, writing of a dream says: 'I shod my feet with the shoes of the lord Hsieh and climbed to Heaven on a ladder of dark clouds.'

---

[88]Raymond Dawson, *The Chinese Experience*, London: Weidenfeld and Nicholson, 1978, p264, note 37, trans. A.M. Lonsdale, cf. J.D. Frodsham, *An Anthology of Chinese Verse*, Oxford, 1967, p135.

He loved mountains, and is said to have regarded himself as a Banished Immortal. He once wrote:

If you were to ask me why I dwell among green mountains,
I should laugh silently, – my soul is serene
The peach blossom follows the moving water:
There is another heaven and earth beyond the world of man.

Bai Juyi, another Tang poet, describes a climb to the Topmost Peak of the Incense-Burner mountain.

He speaks of his delight at being free to go at last, after being detained all the year on official business, and how his soul reeled at the view from the top, the river looking 'narrow as a ribbon' and a castle 'smaller than a man's fist.' On the way home he thought over his experience and realized how difficult it was to shake off 'the dust of the world's halter.' With regret he 'returned to the Ant's Nest.'

The seasonal festivals, symbolism, and rituals of Daoism were designed to ensure harmony between Man and Nature: they acted to prevent disorder 'as dykes prevent floods.' It has been said that the Chinese were the most sophisticated exponents of 'astro-biological' concepts of any people. Similar attitudes appear in the ancient Middle East, India, and South-East Asia: in all these areas, cities, particularly capitals, where divine power was thought to enter the world, were laid out according to a celestial, or cosmic, plan. From the *Book of Songs*:

Splendid was the capital of Shang,
A pattern to the peoples on every side,
Glorious was its fame,
Great indeed its magic power,
Giving long life and peace,
And safety to us that have come after.[89]

[89] *Book of Songs*, trans. Arthur Waley, London: George Allen and Unwin, 1969, p280, No 255.

Man began to make his impact on the environment as soon as the first land was cleared for a temporary camping site. As agriculture developed, sites became more permanent, though slash and burn techniques meant that after some use the land had a chance to recover. In some areas, as, for example the equatorial forests of West Africa, villages became fixed, while areas of forest within reach were utilized in rotation. This method had its limits as with increasing population fertility declined and sometimes the land had to be abandoned. This has been suggested as a possible explanation for the collapse of the Maya civilization in Central America.

Early man everywhere depended on hunting as a supplement to agriculture and ancient China was no exception. In Shang times hunting and fighting became the prerogative of the nobility, while the peasants engaged in agriculture. In the *Book of Songs* the line:

> If you did not hunt, if you did not chase

is followed in three separate verses by the words:

> One would not see all those badgers, the king
> deer, all those quails hanging in your courtyard[90]

or again:

> Shu has gone hunting
> Mounted in his chariot of four
> The reins are in his grasp like ribbons
> While the two outside horses move
> (with regular steps) as dancers do.
> Shu is at the marshy ground
> The fire flames all at once

---

[90] *Book of Songs*, trans. Arthur Waley, London: George Allen and Unwin, 1969, p286, No 259.

And with bare arms he seizes a tiger
And presents it before the Duke.[91]

Fire was used to drive the animals together, and sometimes very large numbers were killed. The highest number recorded in oracle bone inscriptions was 348 Mi deer in one hunt. Methods used included bows and arrows, swords and spears, horses and chariots as well as fire. There were four great seasonal hunts in the year, and the sport was regarded as a good training ground for battle.

The earliest enclosures of wild landscape were for hunting parks. Later came reservations for breeding animals for the hunt, and later still nature reserves and pleasure parks where exotic species of plants and animals could be displayed. The first emperor initiated a park west of the capital Xianyang, as a microcosm of the empire. It contained rare beasts and birds, as well as lakes, farms, and orchards. It was also a hunting preserve.

Large scale hunting must have affected not only the wildlife, but especially when fire was used, the natural vegetation. However, man's responsibility to 'fit in' with nature was not forgotten and hunts were preceded by rituals to appease the spirits of earth and water. A hunting song of Zhou times begins with the verse

A lucky day, fifth of the week;[92]
We have made the sacrifice of propitiation, we have prayed.
Our hunting chariots so lovely,
Our four steeds so strong,
We climb that high hill
Chasing the herds of game.[93]

---

[91] Arthur Waley, *Translations from the Chinese*, London: Visual Publications, 1973, p57–58, quoted from *Chinese Classics: Book of Songs,* trans. J. Legge, Hong Kong, 1871, Vol 4, Part 1, p167–168.
[92] i.e. the 10-day week.
[93] *Book of Songs*, trans. Arthur Waley, London: George Allen and Unwin, 1969, p289, No 262.

The Qin empire was short-lived despite its tremendous effect on the subsequent history of China. The following Han dynasty, which lasted 400 years, built on and expanded the foundations already laid, but eschewed the rigidities and cruelty of the preceding regime, and turned to Confucianism, with its doctrine of the 'superior man' or 'gentleman', who combined learning and refinement with the thrifty simplicity of the farmer, and something of the love of nature of the Daoist. The Han emperors, while the rest of the Court joined in festivities with dancers, jugglers and clowns after great hunting expeditions, retired alone to a tower overlooking the landscape, to commune with the spirits of Nature. The great importance of agriculture was recognized each year when the emperor took on the task of ploughing a symbolic furrow. This attitude persisted down the centuries, with small specimen 'fields' of crops being planted near the Imperial Palace. On the slope of Longevity Hill, in the Summer Palace at Beijing, can be seen the remains of what was in fact a little farm in the days of the Dowager Empress Ci Xi.

The Han emperors took over Shanlin Park, created by Shihuangdi, as a symbol of Empire, and enlarged it to impress visitors from tributary states as well as a site for ritual ceremonies. A wall was built round it extending for over 160km. Five artificial mountains were constructed to represent the five sacred mountains: one in the centre, and one at each of the four corners. Eight rivers converged from the four corners, flowing through forests, plains and gorges, and teeming with fish and turtles. Strange animals were to be seen such as unicorns, 'dragon-bred' horses from Ferghana, rhinoceros and exotic birds from the South. The court poet of the Han emperor Wudi described it thus:

> The sun rises from the eastern ponds
> And sets among the slopes of the west;
> In the southern part of the park,
> Where grasses grow in the dead of winter...
> Live zebras, yaks, tapirs and black oxen,
> Water buffalo, elk and antelope...

Aurochs, elephant and rhinoceros.
In the north, where in the midst of summer
The ground is cracked and blotched with ice...
Roam unicorns and boars,
Wild asses and camels,
Onagers and mares.[94]

Poetic licence no doubt mixes fact and imagination here, but even so, there is no doubt that the park included a great variety of scenery and wildlife. Two lakes were made, and three special islands constructed to represent the three Isles of the Immortals which were thought to exist in the Eastern Sea, but always vanished if they were approached by men. It is possible that the emperor thought that he might be able to entice some Immortals to come and live in his park. The Immortals also were thought to inhabit caves, and holes in rocks. This led later to the craze for bringing strangely shaped rocks, sometimes from great distances, to decorate private gardens. Herbs with medicinal or magic properties, and flowers that bloomed in winter, were another feature of the Imperial Park, which also contained 36 palaces and other buildings. Some officials thought that the emperor had allowed himself to be carried away by his enthusiasm, and had spent far too much money. Many of the nobility created pleasure gardens, some of which were extravagant and ostentatious. The scholar-administrators on the other hand, were often content with much simpler gardens (see Chapter 8). In the third century AD a nobleman who professed Daoist beliefs spent a huge sum of money on an elaborate garden outside the city of Luoyang, the famous Golden Valley Garden. To compete with another garden-maker, he constructed an avenue of brocaded screens 80km long, to outdo that of his rival which extended for 64km!

In 581 AD the son of the founder of the Sui dynasty went to even further excesses. He made a landscape park reminiscent of

---

[94]Maggie Keswick, *The Chinese Garden*, London: Academy Editions, 1978, p34.

that of the Han emperor Wudi: it was 120km round with a lake 10km long connected by waterways to other lakes, to symbolise the five lakes and four seas of the Universe. Sixteen water palaces, each the home of twenty concubines, were built along the waterways. Unusual plants and trees, the latter transported on special carts, were brought from far and wide to furnish the gardens, which were beautified with peach and plum walks. Artificial flowers and leaves of fabric took the place of real ones in winter. Processions of mechanical boats, containing sumptuously dressed wooden figures, 0.6m tall passed along the waterways for the delight of guests.

These extravagances finally bankrupted the dynasty. The founder of the succeeding Tang regime took a very firm line at first, forbidding the digging of ponds and lakes, or the making of gardens. However, he too finally succumbed, and created a great park, the Daminggong, north of the capital Chang'an. It was 64km in circumference and every kind of bird animal and plant could be found there. Separate walled quarters were built, each with its own unique garden. There were facilities for hunting, and a special pavilion was built where the Empress worshipped the goddess of silk. Later in the Tang dynasty the notorious Empress Wu was attracted by the simple life and built a forest retreat about 32km north of the capital. The entire court had to accompany her there, and were forced to sleep in grass huts in great discomfort. This led to a flood of complaints, and in the end the Empress rebuilt the 'retreat' at vast expense. Needless to say, the grateful officials could hardly object!

The first half of the reign of the great emperor Xuanzong (Minghuang) was the 'Golden Age' of the Tang dynasty. The Empire was stable, contacts with other countries were at a peak, and the court was a centre of culture: poetry, music and the arts flourished as never before, or seldom since. The great imperial parks were enlarged. In 740 AD there was a campaign to beautify the cities and the emperor ordered the extensive planting of fruit trees on the roads of the two capitals and in all the parks. He also created a fine herb garden where young men between the ages of 16 and 20 were able to study

ɪuanghe near Zhengzhou, in 1976.

aves in the loess used for storage, between Zhengzhou and Luoyang, in 1976.

Big Wild Goose Pagoda, Xi'an built in 652 AD to house the Buddhist scriptures.

Terraced fields in eastern Sichuan, in 1979.

he division of the Min River at Dujiangyan, in 1983.

assenger steamer on the Yangtze at Badong, in 1979.

Junk on the Yangtze between Wanxian and Qutang, in 1979.

Modern statue of the poet Qu Yuan (340-278 BC) near the East Lake at Wuhan.

rithmetic class in Beijing
ominated by the late
hairman Mao, in 1976.

)ne-child' policy poster in Suzhou, in 1983.

A 'wine-cup stream' at I.M. Pei's Xiang Shan Hote in Beijing, in 1983.

16th century *pailou* on the road to the Ming tombs near Beijing, in 1979.

. *ting* in a garden (Shi Zi Lin) at Suzhou, in 1983.

Iighly Esteemed Rock' in a garden (Liu Yuan) in Suzhou, in 1983.

Thatched peasant house near Chengde, north of Beijing, in 1983.

Karst landscape near Guilin, South China, in 1979.

medicinal herbs of all kinds, and their uses. At this time many plants were being introduced into China from places as far away as Persia, India, and South-East Asia. From about 600 AD, grapes, and wine made from grapes became known in China. In 640 vine cuttings were planted in the Imperial Park, and the Grape Garden was started. Vegetables and garden plants were sometimes requested as 'tribute', and many of these became 'naturalized' in China. Exotic fruits, in particular the famous golden peaches of Samarkand were brought to the capital at great expense, sometimes packed in snow in special containers, as was the case with water-melons.

Unfortunately, the great emperor in the later part of his reign, fell in love with a beautiful concubine, the famous Yang Guifei, and became so enamoured that he almost retired from his state duties. He allowed her large family to invade the court, appointed her relations to important posts, enriched them with money, pavilions and gardens. Her brother with some of his friends made a movable garden on a carriage which rotated as it moved. It was planted with 'renowned flowers and strange trees' and was taken out and displayed to the public in spring.[95] As for Yang Guifei herself, her every wish was gratified by the besotted emperor. At the ancient resort of Huaqing Springs (see p 33) he improved the gardens, and had a tiny island of lapis lazuli built in the lake. Maidservants rowed little boats of sandalwood and lacquer round the island, which represented the acme of aristocratic fashion in gardens at the time. The Emperor and his Court were accustomed to spend the winter at the Floreate Clear Palace which he had built at Huaqing.[96] In 1976 the writer, with other tourists, was shown the 'Concubine's Bath' at the site. It was made of marble with a flower decoration on the base. It is said that the emperor had a small peephole into this little room through which he watched his lady-love being bathed by her

[95]Edward H. Schafer, *The Golden Peaches of Samarkand*, University of California Press, 1985, p121.
[96]Ibid. p233.

handmaidens! In 1989, on the writer's second visit to the springs, enquiries about the Concubine's Bath failed to evince a response. In the early 14th century a poet wrote about a picture he had seen which showed Xuanzong and the Lady Yang on a hot summer day:

> A Gold Millet melon is already split in its basin of ice
> The snowy water is swirled and blended – they try
> the cooling tea.[97]

The date of the picture is unknown: it may be much later than Tang times, but there is evidence of ice pits and ice-urns made of jade, being in use then for the cooling and preservation of food. Yang Guifei is also said to have been very fond of lychees. These grow only in the South of the country, and were brought by post-horse across the whole north-south length of China. A romantic poem by Du Mu refers to this:

> Looking back at Ch'ang-an, an embroidered pile appears;
> A thousand gates among mountain peaks open each in turn.
> A single horseman in the red dust – and the young
> Consort laughs,
> But no one knows if it is the lichees which come.[98]

It appears that the poet had seen the deserted palace at Huaqing, and thought of the courier that brought the lychees from Guangzhou for Yang Guifei.

There is evidence that in Tang times the realization began to dawn that Nature could sometimes be threatened by man. With the enormous growth in literary output the demand for ink increased greatly. The best ink was made from pine soot. A 6th century encyclopedia gives a recipe for one catty (about a lb.) of ink:

---

[97]Ibid. p119.
[98]Ibid. p33.

5 oz pinewood soot strained through silk
5 oz best glue, dissolved in the juice of
the bark of the Ch'in tree
1 oz cinnabar
1 oz musk
5 egg whites.[99]

It became clear that the great demand for pine soot could cause serious deforestation. In the 11th century AD a famous engineer and astronomer suggested the use of petroleum soot as an alternative (see p 55).

Imperial decrees emphasized the respect due to land surrounding temples and royal tombs: such land was 'holy'. Other decrees referred to the danger of fire, forbidding excessive burning of fields, or the lighting of fires near roads. A statement in the Code of Institutes reads:

> On all the five sacred mountains, and on the Notable mountains which are capable of gathering *numina*, and of giving birth to extraordinary things, which can raise clouds and bring rain, having advantage for mankind, all gathering of fuel is interdicted, while prayers and sacrifices shall be made in season 'there'.[100]

Criticism of the extravagances of rulers in the creation of parks and gardens dates back to a thousand years before the Tang dynasty. The philosopher Mencius, in the 4th century BC accused tyrants of turning fields into parks 'thus depriving people of their livelihood'. He points out that 'with the multiplication of parks, ponds, and lakes, arrived birds and beasts', and goes on to describe how the Duke of Zhou had come to the rescue, and 'drove tigers, rhinoceroses, and elephants to the distant wilds, and the Empire rejoiced.'[101] Little did he know

[99]Keith Pratt, *Visitors to China*, London: Macmillan, 1968, Chap 3, p43–44.
[100]Arthur Waley, *Translations from the Chinese*, London: Visual Publications, 1973, p100–101.
[101]*Mencius*, trans. D.C. Lau, (Penguin Classics), Harmondsworth: Penguin, 1970, p113.

how warnings such as his would go unheeded for the next 2000 years, and the passion for landscaping would bring disaster and bankruptcy to one dynasty after another.

Maggie Keswick, in her delightful book, *The Chinese Garden* has this vivid sentence:

> Chinese history is littered with the corpses of gardens ... the end of dynasties has almost inevitably been accompanied by the shrieks of women, the crash of falling rockeries and the crackle of burning pavilions.[102]

The Tang emperor Xuanzong (Minghuang) can be said to have thrown away the Empire for the sake of a woman, but the next great emperor, Huizong of the Song dynasty, sacrificed everything to his passion for landscape gardening. He was one of the most highly cultured of all Chinese emperors, and is famous for his exquisite calligraphy and painting, but also for the great landscaped garden which he created on the flat plain near his capital city of Kaifeng. For many years the 'cosmic garden' had always included rocks to represent mountains, and form a possible habitation for Immortals, but Huizong excelled himself with the building of an artificial mountain rising to 60m above the plain, complete with cliffs, peaks and chasms, and an artificial waterfall. No expense was spared, and it is said that normal traffic on canals and rivers was held up by fleets of barges carrying rocks for the 'mountain'. Tragically, in 1126, the capital and the 'garden' were destroyed by the invading Jurchen Tartars, and Huizong ended his days as a prisoner in a tent in Manchuria.

The city of Hangzhou, and its famous West Lake, now became the capital. Its beautiful surroundings and the prosperity of its inhabitants were described by Marco Polo, who saw it in the days of the Mongol emperor Kublai Khan of the Yuan dynasty, which had succeeded the Southern Song, whose emperors had led a luxurious 'playboy' life in the

---

[102]Maggie Keswick, *The Chinese Garden*, London: Academy Editions, 1978, p47.

splendid palaces and gardens built round the Lake, and in gaily decorated boats hired for sumptuous parties and entertainments. The whole area was in fact, a sort of public park, and as such was greatly enjoyed by the populace of Hangzhou. It had been meticulously cared for and improved during the Tang and Song dynasties. The Tang poet, Bai Juyi, when governor of Hangzhou from 822–824 AD, built a tree-lined causeway which can still be seen today. Strict rules forbade the dumping of rubbish or the growing of water chestnuts in the lake. Buddhist monasteries and temples with their well-kept estates and gardens, as well as the fine houses of noble families, greatly enhanced the beauty of the surrounding hills. The spread of Buddhism in China, and its blending with Daoism, made an important contribution to the development of the Chinese garden. The monastic community, where groups rather than individuals sought enlightenment through contemplation and meditation, was in some ways an enlargement of the concept of the Daoist hermit or the scholar-recluse, and rich men attracted to Buddhism donated money or land for monasteries.

Spring is the recognized season for visiting Chinese gardens, when the flowers are at their best, but the weather in April, though bright and sunny in the north, can be misty and overcast in central China, particularly in Sichuan, and the east coastal areas round the mouth of the Changjiang and Hangzhou. The writer was in Hangzhou in April 1983. The overall impression was of beauty, natural and man-made: scenic beauty glimpsed tantalizingly through veils of mist and light rain, but above all the close-up beauty of flowers and trees, reflections in water, and, unexpectedly beautiful and fantastic fish: huge carp, shoals of normal goldfish, and in the Jade Spring Garden, specially bred freak goldfish in large bowls: some with multiple fins, huge eyes, or complex tails: multi-coloured, and resembling nothing so much as elaborate flowers swimming about. The entire West Lake area is a garden of delight. Dainty pavilions and tea houses merge impeccably with the shapes of islands and rocks, hills and shimmering water. The beauties of the West Lake can best be viewed from an excursion boat. These come in various sizes from the stately, old type 'floating pavilion' roofed in, with carved wooden 'walls', to the smaller versions accommodating up to 20 people. Chinese river and lake excursion boats are a surprise to the Western visitor. They are often roofed with wood or canvas and have open sides, the main body filled by a large rectangular table, complete with chairs. It seems to be assumed that the main object of the trip is food and drink, rather than viewing the scenery. As there is often no standing room, this necessitates taking up a corkscrew attitude in order to enjoy both food and scene. Such boats are to be seen on the Kunming Lake in the Summer Palace in Beijing, and on the Lijiang near Guilin, as well as the West Lake. The larger ones are often towed by small motor boats, while the smaller ones are motor driven. In those used on longer trips the stern area is often taken up by a minute kitchen complete with cooking fire, woks and steamers from which two men will conjure up tasty meals for the passengers. On shorter trips sweets and fruit drinks are served.

The various sites on or near the West Lake have evocative names such as Flower Harbour, Flowery Pond Park, Peony Pavilion, Yellow Dragon Cave. The Flower Nursery has a fine display of table gardens, potted plants and bonsai trees. These dwarfed trees originated in China, and were achieved by slow, highly skilled pruning of roots and branches. They came to the West via Japan, and were assumed to have originated there – hence the Japanese name bonsai. The Wu Hill garden is famous for its bamboos, among them the so-called 'square' bamboos, and for its pebble paving. Paving of elaborate designs has always been a feature of Chinese gardens. At Wu Hill there is a mixture of geometric and natural designs, the latter featuring a pattern of pandas in black, white and grey pebbles. Hangzhou has a fine Botanical Garden, the largest in China, we were told, with many trees labelled with their internationally recognised Latin names. The writer noticed one – 'Fortunei', named after a famous English plant hunter of the late 19th century, Robert Fortune, who brought many specimens back to Kew Gardens, including the lace-bark pine, a 'royal' tree which can be seen in the Imperial Garden of the Forbidden City in Beijing today.

On the eastern shore of the Lake is a path for 'Listening to the Orioles in the Willows'. On the April day when the writer walked it no orioles were singing, and the view across the lake was lost in mist. A pearly opalescent gleam suggested water, against which the willows and the blossoming trees along the path were outlined with the delicacy of a Chinese painting. As we drove back to the hotel, our excellent young Chinese guide, Miss Yu, told us the story of the Phoenix and the Dragon who lived one each side of the Milky Way. They owned, having found, a marvellous stone ground down to a pearl. The Jade Emperor's mother was jealous of this, and stole it. After many vicissitudes, the Phoenix and Dragon retook it, but dropped it as they returned. It fell into a thousand pieces, and became . . . the West Lake!

Not far from the south-west shore of the lake is a famous tea plantation, Meijiawu. In 1983 it was still functioning as a commune. Conditions there are ideal for tea growing, especially the quality of the local spring water from the Dragon Well. It is famous for its special tea, Dragon Well tea, which sells at about six times the normal price. The writer saw some for sale at a Beijing hotel on a previous visit. The cost to tourists was £6–8 a pound in English money. We were told that the Hangzhou tea factory is the largest in China. This best quality tea is picked in spring, when the leaves are most tender, and processed by hand within 24 hours of picking, allowing half an hour at 80°C, and a quarter of an hour at 30°C. Heating is now by electricity, formerly it was by charcoal fire. Leaves picked in summer and autumn are machine-processed. This was taking place in a large barn-like building with a handsome roof of camphor wood whose scent permeated the area.

We also visited the local silk factory, employing 5800 workers, and producing 9.6 million m of silk from 294 tonnes of raw silk each year. Watching the whole process from the boiling of the cocoons to the emergence of the rich brocades, one could only marvel at the patience and ingenuity of the ancient Chinese who produced these wonderful fabrics without benefit of modern machinery or techniques. The intricate designs of the brocades are programmed by rolls of strong paper with punched holes, similar to the 'roll' in a pianola or a circus hurdy-gurdy. Apparently something like this was used in ancient looms. Several years ago a TV programme described how this method came to Europe, and a modern version of it was shown at a silk factory at Lyons. The commentator made the interesting remark that this was, in fact, the ancestor of the former use of punch cards in computers!

The estuary of the Qianting River is notorious for its tidal bore, similar, but on a larger scale, to the Severn Bore in Britain. This often caused serious flooding of the banks in the past, and as a precaution, in 970 AD a pagoda, the Pagoda of the Six Harmonies (speech, body, opinion, mind, wealth, resistance to temptation) was built on the north bank to try to prevent the floods.

The custom of holding Lantern Festivals was revived in 1982, and on our last evening in Hangzhou we were taken to a 'Lantern Show' held in a restored classical garden in the city. It was a fairyland of light and colour: the lanterns, some made by local art students, were hung along the walkways of the garden. They were of every possible size and shape, often highly complex with moving parts controlled by the heat. Cutouts of dragons, warriors in chariots or on horseback, dancers, animals and birds rotated round the central light through miniature landscapes. The climax was a small lake where two splendid red and black dragons, lit from within from head to tail, floated majestically among lotus flowers, and fish in various colours and attitudes, each one a separate lantern.

The splendours of the Song came to an end with the Mongol invasion. In 1215 Genghiz Khan captured Beijing, but it was to take 75 years for the Mongols to take control of the whole country, during which time they became not only civilized but sinicized. Kublai Khan, grandson of the conqueror acceded to the throne in 1260, and became infected with the Imperial craze for building and landscaping. The three lakes in the Parks of the Sea Palaces, west of the Forbidden City in

Beijing, were created by him as was the island in Beihai Park referred to by Marco Polo as the 'Green Mound'. Kublai Khan arranged rocks in his parks: not the limestone of the Chinese gardeners but semi-precious lapis lazuli as used by Xuanzong (Minghuang) at Huaqing Springs. This, with extensive planting of rare trees from all over the country transported by elephants, created a green landscape, 'as green as green can be, and there is no other colour to be seen,' says Marco Polo[103] Kublai also built a summer retreat further north, with a palace and the 'stately pleasure dome' referred to by Coleridge in his poem as 'Xanadu'. This was mobile, and could be set up anywhere in the great hunting park where the emperor liked to enjoy himself away from the summer heat of Cambaluc (Beijing). The Mongol capital described by Marco Polo was built, surprisingly, according to the traditional plan of Chinese cities. Kublai Khan was also responsible for the reconstruction and extension of the Grand Canal to Beijing, which became the main link between north and south China for the next six centuries, emphasising the increasing dependence of the north on the food crops and other products of the centre and south.

The surroundings of imperial tombs were for centuries regarded as holy ground. The tomb of the first Ming emperor (Hongwu 1368–1399) built during his lifetime just outside the capital Nanjing, was finally destroyed during the Taiping Rebellion of 1861, but some ruins, and the sacred way leading to it, can still be seen, flanked by blossoming trees and twelve pairs of large stone animals. Visitors, both foreign and Chinese, delight to climb on them to be photographed, and when the writer saw it in 1983, the whole site was swarming with colourful groups of children climbing over the statues, and sitting on the ground and eating their picnic lunch. School parties visiting ancient sites are a delightful feature of modern China. There is no doubt that the health and well-being of

---

[103] *The Travels of Marco Polo*, trans. R.E. Latham, (Penguin Classics), Harmondsworth: Penguin, 1958, p97.

children is a priority. The 'one-child only' policy, essential to curb the burgeoning population, is often criticized for producing so-called 'little emperors', often spoiled and overfed, or sometimes unduly pressurized by ambitious parents and grandparents. Efforts are being made to compensate for lack of brothers and sisters by encouraging informal play-groups arranged between families, as a supplement to local nursery schools.

In 1421 the capital was moved from Nanjing to Beijing, and the emperor Yongle (1403–1425) set about finding a suitable tomb site for himself and his successors. A beautiful valley north of Beijing was selected, with the help of geomancers. The site was approached by an elaborate sacred way 6km long, bordered by a series of larger-than-life statues: twelve on each side of real or fabulous animals: elephants, camels, horses, and dragons, followed by twelve pairs of human statues: four military men, four officials, and four retainers; symbols of the funeral cortège of an emperor. The tomb of the emperor Wanli (1573–1620) is one of two which have been excavated. It is open to the public and to tourists. Among other treasures 26 chests of jewellery were found, belonging to the two empresses who were interred with the emperor. In 1976 and 1979 much of this, including a superb head-dress decorated with kingfisher feathers were on show in an exhibition building by the tomb exit, but when the writer made a third visit in 1989 most of the contents had been removed, for greater safety, perhaps. An illustration of the Sacred Way in the *National Geographic magazine* for June 1933 shows the statues beside a rough track in a treeless grassy landscape. After 1949 the site was renovated, and a continuous line of trees was planted behind the statues. A newly made road bypasses the handsome five-arched marble *pailou* (gate) built in 1540, which now stands clear of modern traffic. The original Sacred Way was reserved for the emperor and his attendants. Later, one of the Qing emperors wanted to move the statues to the approach to his own tomb, but it is said that one of his ministers dreamed that the statues were loyal to the Ming dynasty, and if they were disturbed a wind of death would blow on Beijing, so the emperor gave up the idea.

The transfer of the capital took some time, and part of the government continued in Nanjing until about 1450. Meanwhile, a new palace and other buildings had been constructed on Kublai Khan's foundations. Today's Forbidden City is mainly Ming in origin and layout, in spite of 300 years of alterations and repairs. The Imperial Garden, with its formal design of raised peony beds, rocks, and ancient trees was also landscaped during the Ming, as was the artificial hill (Coal Hill or Prospect Hill) at the northern end of the complex. This had been built of material excavated when the palace moat was constructed in the 13th century.

Another contribution of the Ming dynasty to the architecture of Beijing was the group of buildings known as the Temple and Altar of Heaven, dated 1420, on a site which was then outside the city. It was described by a visiting architect in 1953 as 'one of the most remarkable architectural compositions in the world. It achieves an overwhelming effect with an extraordinary economy of elements.'[104] Each year the emperor came in solemn procession to perform the ancient rites to ensure a good harvest. He walked from the Temple to the Altar along a rising causeway (360m) which emerged gradually above the tree tops of the surrounding small 'forest' giving the impression that he was leaving the earth to communicate with Heaven. Only men of 70 years of age or more accompanied him to the actual Altar which stood in a circular enclosure within a square. The round Altar was on the highest of three round terraces. Standing on the top induced a feeling of being above the world, as one gazed out on vistas of tree tops in all directions, and felt the force of the old Chinese saying 'The Earth is square, but Heaven is round.' The visiting architect's final words are worth quoting: 'Only a poet could convey the sensation of rising above the earth that one gets on these elevated terraces in their perfect architectural settings surrounded by trees.'[105]

---

[104]Andrew Boyd, *Chinese Architecture and Town Planning 1500 BC–AD 1911*, London: Tiranti, 1962, p140.
[105]Ibid. p142.

The early years of the Ming Dynasty were a time of much economic reconstruction, with a new emphasis on the importance of agriculture as the basis of the nation's resources, and an enthusiasm for reafforestation. In 1391, 50 million trees were planted near Nanjing. Much of this timber was used to build the great ocean-going junks which took part in the voyages of discovery in the Indian Ocean under the famous admiral Zheng He in the 15th century. Knowledge of Chinese civilization spread to South-East Asia, India and even as far as East Africa. Specimens of Ming porcelain dug up near Mombasa can be seen today in the museum at Fort Jesus, the great Portuguese castle on the Kenyan coast. These contacts also greatly increased Chinese knowledge of the world. It is interesting to speculate on what might have been the outcome if the emperor had not cut off financial support for these voyages after 1433, and Zheng He, who wished to sail down the coast of East Africa, had rounded the Cape of Good Hope before Vasco da Gama, who achieved it in 1497–98.

In 1394 landowners were instructed, where space was available to plant 200 mulberries and 200 jujube trees, and two years later, about 84 million fruit trees were called for. During the reign of the first Ming emperor Hongwu (1368–1399) about a 1,000 million trees were planted. However, by the late 16th century, increasing population, and the resulting demand for farming land, led to more forest clearance. In 1580 a law was passed forbidding further tree cutting.

In the 16th century silver coinage was adopted in China, and this had a great effect on population mobility, and the expansion of trade and crafts. Textile, porcelain, and printing, became industrialized for the first time. For many Westerners the word 'Ming' means 'porcelain'. The great centre at Jingdezhen (formerly Ching-te-Chen) reached an all-time high in production in the mid-sixteenth century. Records show that in 1554, 120 thousand pieces were produced for the Court alone, and sent northward by canal in boats specially equipped to carry the fragile cargo. Included were 680 of the famous fish-bowls for watching goldfish, a favourite Chinese pastime. The making of these bowls, which were up to 1m in diameter, called for great skill, as did the firing. The potters faced severe punishment, even death, if a bowl broke, and suicides were not uncommon. According to legend a potter named Cong, at a time when many bowls were broken, threw himself into the furnace. The bowl came out whole. The workmen saw that their luck had changed and built a temple to Cong's memory, where they worshipped him as a god, the God of Fire and Blast. One of these great fishbowls, now in the City Museum and Art Gallery in Birmingham, is described in detail in an article in the *Listener*.[106] The dragon-back kilns of Jingdezhen snaked up the hillsides in accordance with the prevailing wind, to facilitate heating. An old drawing of these can be seen in the museum of Zhenhai Tower in Guangzhou. A group of English potters visited the Jingdezhen area in the 1970s and amazed their Chinese guides by standing up and cheering in their coach when some of the relics came into view. The guides were surprised that the tourists should value such old-fashioned objects in preference to the modern factory, equipped with all the latest machinery. To regard the Ming Dynasty as a Chinese interlude between the two 'foreign' dynasties of the Yuan and the Qing is to underestimate the staying power of Chinese civilization and institutions. The Mongols became sinicized as they spread across the country, and the Manchus, whose invasion ended the Ming dynasty, had already had extensive contact with the many Chinese living in Manchuria. The great river of Chinese civilization has flowed consistently throughout the last 2000 years. The various tributaries which threatened to alter its waters from time to time brought temporary changes, but were finally absorbed into the main stream.

The Qing (1644–1911) dynasty exemplified this, in that the Chinese officials of the Ming were persuaded to continue serving under the Manchus from the beginning of the new dynasty, but it was under the great emperor Kangxi (1661–1722) that this process was completed. A keen scholar himself, the Emperor showed great interest in Chinese classics, and

[106]*Listener*, 23.4.1964, p682–683.

visited the shrine of Confucius in 1684. It is interesting to note that the Manchus never constituted more than two per cent of the total population, but with the alliance of the Court with the official élite, the continuance of Chinese institutions was assured: even so, resistance to the 'foreign' invader smouldered on in the South until it was finally quelled in 1683.[107]

The Qing emperors maintained and improved the palaces and gardens created by the Ming. In 1651 the white marble Dagoba was built on the island in Beihai Park, to celebrate the visit of the Dalai Lama. Mindful of the ever-present danger of invasion from beyond the Great Wall, the Qing emperors endeavoured to consolidate the northern borders and unify the quarrelsome peoples of the steppe by a mixture of diplomacy and military action. Korea and Inner Mongolia were subdued, and Tibet saw the Dalai Lama established as head of state in Lhasa, under the protection of a Chinese garrison. A portrait of the Qing Emperor Qianlong, a symbol of Chinese authority, hangs in the Potala Palace in Lhasa.[108]

Like the Mongols before them, the Manchus found the heat of the Beijing summer oppressive and longed for the cooler air beyond the Great Wall. Emperor Kangxi said: 'When one is beyond the Great Wall the air and soil refresh the spirit ... instead of feeling hemmed in, there is a sense of freedom. It may be the height of summer, but there is dew on the trees ... you have to wear a fur jacket in the mornings.'[109] In common with his Mongol predecessors, he loved hunting, and on one occasion boasted of killing 36 stags in one day 'with gun and bow.' In the 42nd year of his reign he began the construction of a great complex of buildings in a fine park at Jehol, north of the Great Wall, to serve as a summer residence for the Imperial Court. In his private life Kangxi was frugal with public money. His garden in Beijing, though very beautiful,

[107]Yong Yap and Arthur Cotterell, *Chinese Civilization*, London: Weidenfeld and Nicholson, 1977, p74–75.
[108]*China Reconstructs*, February 1981, p68.
[109]Yong Yap and Arthur Cotterell, *Chinese Civilization*, London: Weidenfeld and Nicholson, 1977, p80.

was quite small. The summer residence at Jehol was not just a pleasure park, but a symbol of Imperial authority over the steppe lands.

Now called Chengde, it is the largest imperial garden remaining intact in China. It covers 560 hectares and is surrounded by a wall 10km long. It includes many features reminiscent of Chinese gardening tradition, both north and south. The central feature is a lake beautified by splendid trees, and interspersed with walkways and bridges: a reminder of the West Lake at Hangzhou. In the south-east of the park are the palatial buildings used by the emperor and his court, among them the 'Hall of Simplicity and Sincerity' built of precious *nanmu* wood, brought to the site all the way from Sichuan, near the border of Tibet. It is said that this building alone cost 72,000 taels of silver (about 3 tonnes). After 1711, when the first stages were completed, the Qing court moved to Jehol every summer until 1820, when it was abandoned after the Emperor Jiaqing was killed by lightning near the palace. In 1713 Kangxi began the construction of the 'outer monasteries' to the east and north of the Summer Residence. These were built to emphasize the ties between the court and Lamaist Buddhism. They were completed by the Emperor Qianlong in 1780. Five of the original eight groups remain today, and are well worth a visit. They show an interesting variety of architectural styles, Han Chinese, Mongolian and Tibetan. One of the latter is modelled on the Potala Palace in Lhasa and another on a monastery at Xigazê in Tibet. They were often built to commemorate special occasions, such as the victory of the Emperor in establishing control of the north-west border, the visits of nobles of surrounding tribes, or to congratulate the Emperor on his birthday. The roofs and interiors of the buildings are often splendidly decorated. One roof has 280g of pure gold in the form of gilded copper tiles, with eight gilded copper dragons prancing on the roof ridges.

There were said to be 72 scenes of exquisite beauty in the great park and indeed the writer had the impression of walking among Chinese paintings. In every direction was the backdrop of mountains, while in the foreground bridges and pavilions, rocks and trees, arranged with all the skill of landscape artists, blended with the soft colours of the lake water to give the perfect Chinese definition of landscape (mountain and water). On what is almost an island in the lake is a beautiful little pavilion, the 'Pavilion of the Misty Rain' which was used as a study by Emperor Qianlong. A small white marble table, intricately carved, stands in the centre under the roof. Sitting there in quiet isolation, the Emperor could forget the affairs of state and enjoy the views across the lake. There is a story that the first time he visited this choice little place, it was a hot sunny day, and he was very disappointed that it did not live up to its name. He once said: 'Every emperor and ruler, when he has retired from audience and has finished his public duties, must have a garden in which he may stroll, look around, and relax his heart. If he has a suitable place for this it will refresh his mind and regulate his emotions, but if he has not, he will become engrossed in sensual pleasures, and lose his will power.' He certainly suffered no lack of such places, as he could never resist any suitable garden site. For three years after his accession he restrained himself: partly because he was in mourning for his father, also he did not want to shame his ancestors by committing excesses. He remembered the frugality of his grandfather, Kangxi. Finally, he could resist no longer, and began the extension of the old Summer Palace, the Yuan Ming Yuan. This had been started in the Ming dynasty, and enlarged by the Emperor Kangxi. A description of this splendid garden was sent to Europe in 1749 by Father Attiret, a French Jesuit, and caused a sensation.[110] He described how a complex of formal courtyards and audience halls gave way to a natural scene of 'mountains' (hills 6–15m) covered with flowering trees, streams edged with rocks flowing through small valleys to lakes. He noted more than 200 'palaces' of cedar wood, bridges with white marble balustrades, little menageries, a wealth of fish and aquatic birds, even a small

---

[110]Osvald Sirén, *Gardens of China*, New York: Ronald Press Co, 1949, Chap IX.

'township' complete with walls and gates. He was impressed by the contrast between the formality of Chinese buildings, and the total informality and naturalness of their parks and gardens, where Art had been used to conceal the 'artificial'. All this was such a contrast to the strict formality of French and Italian gardens (he had Versailles in mind), that it struck him, and many who read his description, with the intensity of a totally new way of looking at the natural world, and man's place in it. In Europe man seemed intent on mastering Nature; in China he worked with Nature: this was Daoism.[111] Father Attiret confessed that perhaps his eyes and ears had indeed become 'a little Chinese', as he had come to admire that which at first had seemed odd and meaningless. His attitude struck a chord in England, where gardens were less formal than in Europe. About that time, Alexander Pope was planning a new house and garden and is said to have remarked that 'One must consult the Genius of the Place.'[112] Qianlong saw to it that every aspect of Chinese traditional gardens should be represented in the Yuan Ming Yuan, including a miniature street of shops, a rice-field, and a mountain village. He was shown pictures of the palace and gardens at Versailles by French Jesuit priests, and decided to commission buildings and gardens in the same style to be constructed on the northern edge of the Yuan Ming Yuan. They were built between 1747 and 1760, having been designed by an Italian Jesuit and his colleagues.

In October 1860 the whole wonderful complex was sacked, looted, and burned by a combined force of British and French troops to 'teach the Chinese to see reason.'[113] On the 120th anniversary of the destruction in 1980 a Yuan Ming Yuan society was formed to initiate the restoration of the garden. Fortunately there are many records of the original, the plans

---

[111]Ibid.
[112]Maggie Keswick, *The Chinese Garden*, London: Academy Editions, 1978, p15.
[113]*China Reconstructs*, February 1981, p43.

of pools and streams are still in existence, and 150 of the artificial 'hills' are still intact. The writer visited the site in 1983. Among the long grass and rough ground, many pieces of broken marble and carved tiles reveal glimpses of the lost beauty.

Among the debris the writer saw a broken slab of marble showing the remains of a curved channel cut in the stone, and realized that it was a fragment of a Liu Shui Yin, or 'wine-cup stream'. Earlier in the day we had visited the new Xiang Shan Hotel, west of Beijing, built in the early 1980s by the famous Chinese-American architect I.M. Pei, designer of the 'glass pyramid' at the Louvre, as well as some well-known buildings in the USA. He had hoped to stimulate a return from high-rise hotels and flats to a more traditional style of Chinese architecture, and had incorporated into the hotel and its garden many characteristic features such as shaped windows, ornamental paving, rocks, trees, and water, and a Liu Shui Yin.[114] This dates back to the 'Gathering at the Orchid Pavilion' in April 353 AD, when a group of poets gathered by a stream to celebrate the Water Festival. They floated cups of wine in paper boats down a stream for a distance of about 50m. The 'game' which became a popular pastime, was to complete a poem before the wine-cup reached its destination. Failure to do so meant forfeiting the wine. Many such man-made wine-cup streams became features in the gardens of the upper classes. The sight of the broken fragment in the ruins of the Yuan Ming Yuan was a poignant reminder of the tragedy of October 1860, when not only was an exquisite garden destroyed, but also a complete library of the Chinese classics, housed in one of the fine buildings.

Qianlong promised that the Yuan Ming Yuan would be the last of his extravagances. He said that with so many splendid parks and gardens, his descendants would be spared the expense of creating more: but the expansion of Chengde and

---

[114]Thomas Hoving, 'More than a Hotel', *Connoisseur*, February 1983, p68–81.

the developments in the Fragrant Hills west of Beijing followed.[115] He just could not resist the opportunity to create a landscape. To the west of Beijing a large park had been formed when the Jade Spring was dammed to supply water to the Forbidden City and its lakes. Qianlong used this lake (Lake Kunming) for naval training for a time, but noticing the enchanting view across the lake to the Western Hills, he began to think of creating yet another great park. His mother's 60th birthday in 1750 gave the opportunity. She, like her son, was a great admirer of the beautiful city of Hangzhou and its West Lake, and the Emperor decided to make a replica at Lake Kunming as a birthday present for her. Pavilions and walkways were built, and an artificial island, the Island of the Dragon King, linked to the shore by the seventeen-arch bridge, enhanced the beauty of the lake. In a secluded area on the north-east Qianlong created a small secret garden, the 'Garden of Harmonious Interest', based on a lovely old garden at Wuxi, which he had visited. This beautiful little spot is an ideal retreat from the crowds of tourists who frequent the Summer Palace. Round the garden tall trees give a feeling of seclusion. The tiny lake is encircled by walkways with little pavilions, in one of which is an upright stone slab embellished by the beautiful calligraphy of Emperor Qianlong. The writer visited it on two occasions, in spring when it was resplendent with the dazzling white of the magnolias and the green veils of the willows, and a party of small school children sat by the lake eating their picnic lunch, their bright clothes adding to the gaiety of the scene: and in winter, when the roofs of the walkways and pavilions were white with frost and the low winter sun lit up the red pillars and decorated eaves, giving a horizontal dimension to the scene which was quite absent in spring, when the buildings appeared taller. The buildings along the shore of Lake Kunming were destroyed in 1860, at the time of the sack of Yuan Ming Yuan and the Dowager Empress Ci

[115]Maggie Keswick, *The Chinese Garden*, London: Academy Editions, 1978, p66.

Xi was about to celebrate her 60th birthday, in honour of which she decided to undertake repairs, and promised to revive Qianlong's idea of a naval training base on the Lake. A foreign loan was raised for this purpose, and many rich Chinese donated money. In the end there was no naval base, but the set of buildings known as the New Summer Palace, and the extravaganza known as the Marble Boat at the western end (see p 72). Nemesis came in 1894–1895, with the Sino-Japanese war, when for want of a modern navy China suffered a humiliating defeat. However, an old gardener is said to have remarked: 'Look! ... who would ever have thought that such beautiful things could be made by the hands of men, had she not spent the money on it?'[116]

Since 1949, in spite of the chaotic years of the Cultural Revolution (1966–1976), the restoration and maintenance of China's ancient parks and gardens has continued. Many are now open to the public and to foreign visitors, for whom a 'Garden Tour', accompanied by a knowledgeable guide, is a very worthwhile experience.

During the communist years, educational exhibitions became a feature of many public parks: to quote just two examples: the People's Cultural Park in Beijing, a 'twin' to the east of the Zhongshan Park, has some fine buildings which once contained the Imperial Ancestral Tablets. Some of these now form a school, and another an Exhibition Hall. A smaller building displays posters giving details of training for various careers such as nursing and teaching. In Guangzhou a much larger 'cultural' park includes a feature describing fishing in the South China Sea, with an excellent diorama, maps, and models of boats and tackle, and many preserved fish in jars, well labelled for the use of visiting school parties and students. Adjoining this is a botanical exhibition, with four rooms representing the four seasons, each with many specimen live plants, supplemented by drawings and paintings of others which are

[116]Ibid. p72, quoted from Su Hua, *Ancient Melodies*, London: Hogarth Press, 1969, Chap 12, p169.

not on show. There is also an aquarium, and in an outside courtyard a goldfish pond with a porcelain dolphin fountain in the centre. The writer visited this park on October 2nd 1979, China's National Day. It was packed with people and beautifully decorated.

8

THE COSMIC LANDSCAPE II
Gardens of Poets, Painters, and Scholars

In the previous chapter we have been concerned with the gardening, or rather the landscaping, activities of the Emperors, and the very wealthy for whom expense was hardly a consideration. Indeed, Imperial parks were often ostentatious, and aimed at impressing foreign visitors. However the Daoist conception of Man and his place in the natural environment was always present to some degree. In the private gardens of the educated élite, the scholars, painters, and poets steeped in the classical culture of China, this emphasis predominated. During time off, or in retirement from their official duties in the Civil Service, they enjoyed cultural pursuits such as painting, and poetry, music and the creation of gardens. These varied with the wealth and taste of their owners. Some were private family estates, where house and garden were integrated: in cities these were usually separated from the public by high walls. The country cottage or 'rustic retreat of the scholar' often consisted of a small thatched cottage surrounded by a garden to which the owner could retire from his busy city life to meditate, commune with Nature, write poetry or paint; sometimes in solitude, sometimes in the company of friends who shared the same background. All members of the 'literati', the scholar-gentry, had had the traditional classical education, and sat for the Civil Service examinations, which determined their official status. Friendships made during these early years often endured a lifetime. This cohesion of age-groups among men is world-wide, from the 'Old Boy Network' and the year groups of University alumni to the tribal hierarchies of the Masai 'moran' or warriors of East Africa.

Busy officials often found themselves isolated in a city far from home, with little opportunity to visit the countryside. For them a landscape painting or a desk garden could be a substitute, a small model containing all the essentials of the Chinese landscape in miniature: rocks, water, trees and flowers, pavilions and bridges. This model garden on a tray, stood on the desk along with the other accoutrements of a scholar:[117] brushes for calligraphy and painting: these were of bamboo with various tips of rabbit, deer or goat hair: ink sticks, an inkstone and water dropper, seals carved from ivory, and a paper knife. Larger miniature gardens were often displayed in the house on shelves or tables. These frequently included the dwarfed trees described on p 122.

In his translation of the poetry of Li Bai (701–762 AD) Arthur Cooper comments that 'Home, sweet Home' is one of the chief themes of all Chinese poetry, and is often expressed as a longing for a lost garden, as in this example: *On Hearing a Flute on a Spring Night at Luoyang*:

> From whose house is it a clear flute
> in the dark so flies its voice
> it intermits Spring winds
> filling Lo city?
>
> For this evening among its airs
> hearing 'Breaking the Withies',
> who will not remember
> long ago gardens?[118]

---

[117]Keith Pratt, *China Past and Present*: Filmstrip No 7, Visual Publications, London, 1973, Note on frame 13.
[118]Arthur Cooper, *Li Po and Tu Fu*, (Penguin Classics), Harmondsworth: Penguin, 1973, p107.

(An air for the flute, referring to the custom of breaking off withies from the willows on the riverbank by a bridge outside the city of Chang'an, as a symbol of reluctant parting; 'Long ago gardens' means one's old home.)

Landscape painting, poetry, calligraphy, and garden design were all linked in the Daoist attitude to Nature. In meditating on the natural environment the Daoist attempted to become one with the Qi, the life-force which lay behind the cosmos. The aim was to seek the inner harmony and meaning of both Nature and Man. A Chinese landscape painting was in no sense a 'picture' in our meaning of the word. It was intended to express the essence of the scene as it emerged from the perception of the painter. The same brushes were used for painting and calligraphy, and the brush strokes were said to embody the 'energy of a living thing.' The 'characters' of Chinese calligraphy often carried a rich symbolism, and varied shades of meaning, which made them a sort of artistic shorthand. It was said that printed characters were stiff, but the brush 'danced', so painters who were also calligraphers learned by watching Nature in the flowing of water, the flight of birds or the shadows of bamboo moving on a white wall in the moonlight.

For the educated Chinese, this intense communion with Nature took the place occupied by religions in other cultures. It was expressed in various artistic activities, as well as in meditation and contemplation and was not without essential rituals. Poems were often added to landscape paintings to augment, by calligraphy and words, the impression made by the painting. Gardens were sometimes regarded as three-dimensional paintings. It has been said that the Chinese 'reached the greatest heights of philosophical and imaginative experience of landscape'[119] of any people, and that the scholar officials were arbiters of taste and the largest group of art patrons that the world has known.

In his *Essay on Landscape Painting* written in the 11th

[119]Raymond Dawson, *The Chinese Experience*, London: Weidenfeld and Nicholson, 1978, p205.

Century AD, Guo Xi asks,[120] 'Why does the virtuous man take delight in landscape?' and answers: 'In rustic retreat he may nourish his nature, amid streams and rocks, take delight, meet fishermen, woodcutters, hermits, see soaring cranes, hear monkeys crying,' and goes on to say that if a man is so busy that he can see natural landscapes only in dreams 'How delightful then to have a landscape painted by a skilled hand.'

He then discusses the importance of the painter's attitude if he is to communicate the inner meaning or the essence of the landscape to the man looking at the painting. The painter must concentrate on the essential nature of the landscape: if he fails to do this, he will not present the 'soul' of the scene. Depth of meaning cannot be conveyed without discipline on the part of the painter, who needs to approach his subject with reverence and diligence. Guo Xi describes how his father, when he was about to paint, insisted on a bright window and an orderly desk, with incense burning on the right and left, and best quality brushes and ink. He would wash his hands, rinse out the ink container, and work 'as if guarding against a strong enemy.' As for himself Guo Xi adds, 'Unless I dwell in peace and sit in leisure with windows cleaned, the desk dusted, incense burning, and ten thousand worries drowned and subdued, I am not able to get at the mood and meaning of beautiful lines, think excellent thoughts, or imagine the subtle feelings described in them. The same thing is true of painting.'

He continues with advice to the painter of landscapes. He must identify himself with the scenes, take note of the seasons, observe wind and rain, become aware of changes in atmosphere when rain is approaching, clearing away or falling heavily. Above all, he must be the master and not the slave, of brush and ink. This will involve years of discipline and practice. Perhaps one could compare this with the effort required of a skilled musician in modern times. He must

[120]Kuo Hsi, *Essay on Landscape Painting*, trans. Shio Sakanisi, London: John Murray, 1935.

become the complete master of his instrument practising tirelessly until he reaches that breakthrough point where mistakes become almost unthinkable, and the path from brain through hand to instrument is totally clear, so that interpretation is all and practical problems cease to exist. This appears most obvious in works of great genius. Michelangelo chipping frantically at a block of marble to release his vision of the finished statue or Chopin struggling to write his music alone in his room, often refusing food, and surrounded by a debris of broken pens and torn paper. Such birth-pangs are part of Nature from the survival of the species to the creation of works of art of every kind.

Guo Xi's essay is as relevant today as it was 900 years ago. He comments that 'poetry is a picture without form,' and 'painting is a poem with form.' Here are two of his quotations:

> The bamboo thicket sieves the raindrops
> The high peak holds the evening glow

by Xiahou Shujian, and a verse by Du Fu:

> Painting only one stem in five days
> And only one stone in ten days
> Refusing to yield to compulsion and pressure
> Wang Tsai was willing to hand down his master strokes.

Garden design followed the principles applied to landscape painting, attempting to express the feeling for Nature in a realistic way, using rocks, water, trees and flowers interspersed with paths, bridges and pavilions to create an experience similar to that enjoyed on an excursion into the natural landscape. Flower beds, the main feature of many European gardens, played only a minor part in many Chinese gardens, though blossoming trees were greatly valued. Lawns were entirely absent, flat spaces being often paved with intricate designs of pebbles. Maggie Keswick quotes an amusing comment by a Chinese visitor to England in the 1920s: 'a mown bordered lawn, while no doubt pleasing to a cow, could hardly engage the intellect of human beings.'[121] Even quiet small gardens were planned to offer a series of surprises, hidden scenes to be enjoyed in sequence along a prescribed route.

In his fascinating book *Scholar Gardens of China*, R. Stewart Johnston describes an exquisite tiny garden in Suzhou.[122] Covering only 132m^2 it contains a small pavilion high up in one corner, from which one looks down on a rock grotto, and a lake surrounded by trees and flowers, all connected by winding paths giving different views, and a wooden stairway leading up to the main viewpoint. He quotes a poem by Tang Yin (1470–1524 AD):

> Jade-fresh bamboos,
> Rare-shaped stones,
> Blue ancient pines,
> Old gnarled branches –
> Sighting all these,
> Through a window,
> On a fine day,
> What a joy![123]

To view the whole garden from a single window or balcony was possible only in the smallest gardens, and was not considered desirable. The larger the area available, the greater the number of 'secret' views which could be arranged, and a walk through one of the beautifully restored ancient gardens of Suzhou brings to the modern traveller something of the experience of the scholar-gardener. It can be compared to the unrolling of a scroll painting, or in some ways to listening to a symphony, and becoming aware of the changes in the mood in the successive movements. It is possible on turning an abrupt

[121] Maggie Keswick, *The Chinese Garden*, London: Academy Editions, 1978, p18.
[122] R. Stewart Johnston, *Scholar Gardens of China*, Cambridge: CUP, 1991, p173 and 168.
[123] Ibid. p166; 'A Vista,' quoted from Lai T'ien Chang, *T'ang Yin: Poet/Painter, 1470–1524*, Hong Kong: Kelly & Walsh, [1971], p87.

corner in a zigzag walkway, or passing through a moon gate to a fresh garden, to have the illusion of a change in background music, though in fact there is none: so closely connected are our perceptions of light and sound, colour and form, or as the garden designer would have said, the 'Qi', the 'Life movement of the Spirit through the rhythm of things.'

In the long tradition of Chinese garden-making the ingredients hardly varied except in quantity, which of course depended on the area available and the wealth of the owner. The table garden on the desk of the city-bound official was essentially the same as the rustic plot surrounding the thatched cottage of his country retreat. From the earliest, rocks and water, representing the basic landscape, were the main features, and 'petromania', the passion for collecting unusual rocks, became an obsession of all gardeners from Emperor to civil servant. The great 17th century 'Manual of Gardening' the *Yuan Ye* has a detailed chapter on the selection of rocks: they should 'appear wild': single rocks should be thin at the base, thus appearing to 'float'. However it concluded that 'in creating works of art, the man is of far greater importance than the material, however valuable this may be.'[124] The most sought-after specimens were dredged up from Taihu, the large lake near Suzhou, and were formed of limestone, worn into strange shapes by the action of water. The more crevices, twists and holes the better; in earlier times these were regarded as possible dwelling places for Immortals. Sometimes the rocks were worked on, chiselled and polished by craftsmen to improve the appearance, and even put back in the lake for a time for Nature to finish the job. An eccentric 11th century artist Mi Fu (1051–1107 AD) used to commune on his knees with a special rock in his garden addressing it as 'Elder brother'. He initiated an impressionistic type of painting called 'Mi-dots', where he used the side of the brush to make small blobs: he is also reported to have worn Tang dynasty dress.

[124]Osvald Sirén, *Gardens of China*, New York: Ronald Press Co, 1949, Chap I.

The centre-piece and focus of many gardens was water, usually in the form of a lake or pool, sometimes a stream: this was often planted with lotus, the symbol of purity, friendship and peace; and enlivened with carp or goldfish. The surroundings of the lake were always carefully designed to make the most of the effects of water at different seasons, and different times of the day and night, particularly at times of full moon. In treatises on gardening it was advised that in the first views of the lake the limit should not be in sight, but 'hidden' behind an island, or round a corner, thus enhancing the feeling of mystery, with surprises yet to come, essential to a well planned garden.

Sometimes the family dwelling was beside the water. In any case, the lake was the focus of walkways and bridges, interspersed with viewpoints and small pavilions, built out over the lake to take advantage of summer breezes, to enable close-up views of the lotus, and enjoyment of its scent or to observe the movements of fish. In more secluded areas were library or study pavilions where the scholar could work or read in peace, surrounded only by Nature. Flowers and trees often had symbolic significance. The plum, the pine and the bamboo were the 'Three friends of winter', the plum blossom being the herald of spring, the pine representing dignity and strength. The Tang poet, Bai Juyi, once bought a house simply on account of ten pine trees growing in a courtyard. He wrote a poem about this:

At each season they have their varying mood;
Vying in this with any tree that grows.
Last year, when they heard I had bought this house,
Neighbours mocked and the World called me mad –
That a whole family of twice ten souls
Should move house for the sake of a few pines!
Now that I have come to them, what have they given me?
They have only loosened the shackles that bind my heart.
But even so, they are 'profitable friends',
And fill my need of 'converse with wise men'.
Yet when I consider how, still a man of the world,

In belt and cap I scurry through dirt and dust,
From time to time my heart twinges with shame
That I am not fit to be master of my pines![125]

The poet Tao Yuanming (Tao Qian) (370?–427 AD) worked reluctantly for a long time as a minor official but finally returned to his country retreat, where he took up farming. He wrote of his pleasure of rambling round his garden, often lingering until sunset, 'Caressing with my hands a solitary pine.'[126] He was famed for his passion for chrysanthemums. These flowers were the symbol of autumn, defying the frosts, and representing survival. More than a thousand years later the artist Chen Hongshou (1599–1652) painted a hand scroll to illustrate Tao Yuanming's long poem *Homecoming*, in which he depicts the poet sitting on a rock, enjoying the scent of a bunch of chrysanthemums. Beside him are a lute and a bowl of wine, representing the poet's main interests apart from his garden.[127]

In the late autumn of 1976, just after the death of Mao Zedong, the writer saw massed chrysanthemums in public parks placed around his portrait, white flowers predominating, as white is the colour associated with funerals in China. Apart from these special displays, it was interesting to see many 'trained chrysanthemums', where the plants were grown as bushes, each flower stalk being wired to produce an almost smooth hemispherical surface of blooms of equal size and maturity, the largest 'bushes' being about one metre in diameter. It was difficult to tell how this had been achieved, and the guide could not explain it. There were some fine specimens decorating the main platform of Guangzhou station. The traditional dwarfing of trees (bonsai) has already been

[125]Arthur Waley, *Chinese Poems*, London: George Allen and Unwin, 1961, p156.

[126]Arthur Waley, *Translations from the Chinese*, London: Visual Publications, p123.

[127]James Cahill, *Chinese Painting*, (Treasures of Asia Series), London: A. Skira Macmillan, 1977, p156.

mentioned, and from time to time, in public gardens, trees were sometimes trained into fantastic shapes, young trunks, branches, and even roots twisting into corkscrews, or grown to represent a deer and its antlers, or trimmed and wired into the exact shape of an umbrella. This tampering with Nature, as with breeding of strange goldfish, was accepted as part of man's 'communion' with the Qi, or life-force. The development of dwarf trees took place to enable the city-bound official to enjoy a representation of wild nature on his office desk, or in his town house.

There was some massed planting of flowers often in raised beds. The peony the 'King of Flowers' was one of the few examples of this type of display. The Imperial Garden in the Forbidden City in Beijing is famous for its beds of tree peonies, a variety at one time reserved for the Emperor. On the south-west shore of the West Lake at Hangzhou is Peony Pavilion, which has a splendid display in early summer.

Blossoming trees and shrubs played an important role in Chinese gardens, and were often placed in positions where their seasonal display would add to the interest of the garden. The writer saw a good example of this at the Summer Palace in Beijing, where a small courtyard barely noticed on a previous visit in late autumn, was transformed in April by a dazzling display of pure white magnolias.

Plum and apricot were often used in this way, but the favourite for both fruit and flowers was the peach. This had traditional significance because of the ancient legend of the peaches of longevity which were said to ripen every 3000 years in the Daoist Garden of the Queen Mother of the West. To eat them was to become an Immortal. The poet Tao Yuanming (Tao Qian), told in prose and verse a tale that became well known among educated Chinese, the famous 'Tale of the Peach Blossom Spring'. A fisherman, wandering upstream, found himself in a forest of peach trees, which ended at the source of the stream. Here he noticed a small opening in the rocky hillside, so he tied up his boat, and decided to explore further. The narrow opening broadened into a cave, and on reaching the mouth, he saw laid out before him, a landscape of rice-fields and bamboos, houses and other buildings, with many people going about their business, and heard the sounds of dogs and fowls. He went down among them and saw that they were dressed in clothes unfamiliar to him, and that everyone appeared happy and prosperous. They received him hospitably, gave him a meal and gathered round him, showing great interest, and enquiring whence he came. They explained that their ancestors had fled the upheavals of the Qin dynasty, and had become isolated in this valley, hence their strange ancient type of clothing. The fisherman spent several days in this idyllic place, and then went back to his boat and made his way home, where he reported his discovery to the authorities, having made careful note of all the features of the route. It was decided that he should return to the valley, accompanied by a man appointed by the local Prefect. They set off, but in spite of him having noted every detail the fisherman could not find the way. Later a well-known man of Nanyang offered to go but died before he could begin the journey.[128] No one else attempted it, but the story became part of the literary background, and references to it abound in painting and poetry, where one only has to see the words 'peach petals or peach blossom' to realize a possible link with the ancient tale. Here are a few examples: Li Bai, in the poem quoted (on p 111) where he says:

The peach blossom follows the moving water

Wang Wei (699–761 AD) another great Tang poet who was also a painter, wrote a poem (about the story) when he was 19 ending with these words:

But how many green streams lead into cloud-high woods –
When spring comes, everywhere there are peach
blossom streams
No one can tell which may be the spring of paradise.

---

[128] *Poems of Wang Wei*, trans. G.W. Robinson, (Penguin Classics), Harmondsworth: Penguin, 1973, p34–36 and Appendix II.

Also in a poem entitled *The Monastery of the Stone Gate in the Lantian Hills* in which he describes the discovery of an isolated group of priests who had lost touch with the world:

> Not to risk losing the way there on a second search
> I should be up at daybreak to climb that way again
> Good-bye, friends of Peach Tree Spring
> When the flowers are red I shall be there once more.[129]

High mountain regions, such as the Himalaya, or the Sino-Tibet border, have always suggested mystery, with the possibility of strange survivals such as the Abominable Snowman (Yeti), or lost communities, free of the usual troubles of mankind, where people live peacefully to a great age, and are often in possession of fundamental religious truths denied to the rest of the world. Even today, people make pilgrimages to places like Ladakh in the hope of finding Utopia, Shangri-La, or a lost Paradise. The tale of the Peach Blossom Spring is a Chinese version of a universal human longing.

The Chinese have a great love and respect for trees, especially when they are old and gnarled, like the 1000-year-old cypresses in the Forbidden City or the ancient gingko trees which inspired the design of the garden of the Xiang Shan Hotel in the hills west of Beijing. The sophora was known as the 'Scholars' tree'. The entrance to the Imperial Garden in the Forbidden City is through a natural arch formed by two sophora trunks which have apparently grown together: or maybe both were originally part of the same tree. Another well-known flowering tree is the osmanthus, possibly the Gui from South China. It is planted along the main street of Guilin, which became known as the 'city of osmanthus trees', and is famous for its wonderfully scented blossom, which fills the air in spring. The writer enjoyed it by the East Lake in Wuchang in the Spring of 1979, where the enchanting scent was reminiscent of that of the 'temple tree' (frangipani) of

---

[129]Ibid. p38.

India. A sprig of osmanthus in a lidded basket brought home by the writer caused a minor sensation at Heathrow, where there was suspicion of cannabis smuggling! Incidentally, something of the scent persisted for almost a year.

In addition to basic essentials of rocks, water, trees, and flowers, no Chinese garden was complete without buildings, paths and bridges, and these varied with the wealth of the owner, from the simple *ting*, a small open pavilion for viewing and resting, to the grand reception hall, or the multi-storied *lou*. Libraries of all sizes were often included, as were studies, and studios for painting. Windows, often shaped to represent flowers, were so placed as to 'frame' garden scenes. Some were latticed in various patterns, others were partially filled in with carved silhouettes. Walls, doors, and openings such as moon-gates defined the various sections of the garden. Because evil influences were thought to prefer travelling in straight lines, paths and bridges often zigzagged or turned frequently. Maggie Keswick quotes a saying, 'Once a place has a t'ing we can call it a garden.'[130] In the same book page 163 is an illustration of the famous historian Sima Guang, sitting in a home-made *ting* which he constructed on an island, by tying together the tops of a circle of bamboos. Here he was surrounded by his herb garden, divided into 120 small squares containing various kinds of medicinal herbs, all labelled. He also had six enclosures for peonies and other flowers, two specimens of each, labelled. His famous garden, the 'Garden of Solitary Enjoyment', was made when he retired from official work to write his history. It was '*rus in urbe*' a simple country retreat in the city, the only expensive feature being a library to house his 5000 books.[131]

An interesting feature of viewing pavilions and terraces is that the seating faces inwards, but the sloping back-rest facili-

---

[130]Maggie Keswick, *The Chinese Garden*, London: Academy Editions, 1978, p119.

[131]Osvald Sirén, *Gardens of China*, New York: Ronald Press Co, 1949, Chap V.

tates viewing, and makes it easy to look down on lotus or fish in nearby water. Internal furniture in garden pavilions is simple and elegant and often finely carved, and consists mainly of tables and chairs and stands for potted plants or vases. Paintings of landscapes or flowers often adorn the walls. Sometimes mounted tablets display comments on the garden, or original poems by visitors, or quotations from literature.

In Cao Xueqin's novel, *The Story of the Stone*, generally known as *A Dream of Red Mansions* there is a detailed account of the building of a garden for the Jia family. When it is completed the leading members of the family walk round it, and there is much discussion about suitable inscriptions to be displayed on boards, labelling the buildings and the different sections of the garden. Twenty to thirty names were suggested, often by literary friends of the owner, but some by his eldest son, subjected to what amounted to a test of his knowledge of literature. Inside the entrance to the garden was an artificial hill greatly admired by the party, one of whom said that without it the whole garden would have been visible at the beginning, and 'all its mystery would be lost.'[132]

There could be no greater contrast to this very expensive garden than that of the Tang poet and scholar Bai Juyi, who in the autumn of 817 AD found a site below the Incense Burner Peak and built himself a cottage as a rural retreat. Before he began he sacrificed to the spirits of the mountain, asking their permission, entreating them to 'see to it that I encounter no hobgoblins, wild beasts or poisonous snakes, but that these may all keep themselves to themselves.'[133,134] The cottage was small, with two rooms and four windows, its woodwork unpainted and its walls not whitewashed. Furniture consisted of four simple wooden beds, two plain screens, a few books

---

[132]Cao Xueqin, *The Story of the Stone*, Vol I, trans. David Hawkes, (Penguin Classics), Harmondsworth: Penguin, 1973, Introd p19 and Chap 17.

[133]Arthur Waley, *Life and Times of Po Chü-i*, London: George Allen and Unwin, 1970, p118–119.

[134]Osvald Sirén, *Gardens of China*, New York: Ronald Press Co, 1949, Chap V.

(Confucian classics, Daoist and Buddhist scriptures) and lacquered lutes. In the open area in front was a flat terrace and a square pool planted with white lotus, and containing white fish for the table. The poet made a path of white stones under a group of pine trees. He referred to the cottage as a 'grass hut', and on the day he moved in, he sat enthralled by the view of mountains, torrents, ancient pines, from the hour of the Dragon (7am) to the hour of the Cock (5pm). Sometime later he gave a house warming party for 22 friends, and the guests included several monks from the Forest Temples nearby. Tea and fruit were served in place of wine and meat, in keeping with the vows of the monks. The next day he wrote a letter to an old friend telling him that 'Everything that has always given me most pleasure is to be found in this place ... I would be content to stay here until the end of my days.'[135]

Suzhou is the city where the Art of old Chinese gardens can be seen at its best today. Indeed the city itself still preserves enough of its ancient beauty and interest to tempt the modern traveller interested in China's past. It became a favourite venue for retired officials, most of whom were scholars, painters or poets, who bought land and created gardens in the classical tradition. About twenty of these still exist, and some have been carefully restored and are now open to the public. It is worth quoting an old Suzhou poet's attitude to the viewing of a garden:

> One should have a knowledge of the historical background: one should enter the garden in a peaceful and receptive mood: one should use one's observation to note the plan and pattern of the garden, for the different parts have not been arbitrarily assembled, but carefully weighed against each other like the pairs of inscribed tablets placed in the pavilions. And when one has thoroughly comprehended the tangible forms or objects, one should endeavour to attain an inner communion with the

[135]Ibid.

soul of the garden, and try to understand the mysterious forces governing the landscape and making it cohere.[136]

Thus it appears that a visit to a garden can be more than an artistic experience, similar to the unrolling of a scroll painting, but touches something fundamental in that one becomes aware of the Qi, the life-force which permeates and controls all the beauty and variety of the planet. This feeling will only be available to the visitor where the creator of the garden has been imbued with the same sentiments (see p4 of Guo Xi's instructions to the landscape painter).

One of the best examples of a classic garden in Suzhou is the Wang Shi Yuan, known as the 'Garden of the Master of the Nets' or the 'Fisherman's Retreat'. It was created first 800 years ago, in 1140 AD by a high official of the Song court, who called it the 'Hall of Ten Thousand Books'. After his death there is an incredible gap of 600 years until 1770 when it was taken over by another official who named it the 'Fisherman's Retreat', to signify that hence forward he intended to lead a quiet life, free from politics.[137]

Various owners followed him, and the garden flourished during the later years of the Qianlong period (up to 1796 AD), a time of great interest and achievement in garden design. Today it covers an area of approximately 0.4 hectares, and is noted for the skilful use of limited space, in which there is no feeling of overcrowding. A modern Chinese writer has described it as a perfect example of the classical tradition in that it avoids over-large buildings, bridges, or rock-piles, and all its features are the correct size for a small garden.[138] Everything is kept to a suitable scale, so that one has the impression of adequate space. The house, in accordance with tradition, is separated from the garden, and occupies the south-east quarter

---

[136]Ibid. p94.
[137]R. Stewart Johnston, *Scholar Gardens of China*, Cambridge: CUP, 1991, p111.
[138]Ibid. p123 (see comment to 122).

of the area, with the main halls along the traditional north-south axis. Two of the four garden entrances communicate directly with the residential area, giving private access for the family and their guests. The garden contains a number of other buildings including a music room, library plus study, two lakeside pavilions, and a tiny private study with its own small garden in the north west corner. All are linked by walkways which encircle the lake at varying levels, and provide a panorama of rocks, trees, flowers and buildings reflected in the clear water of the lake. To enhance the sense of space the lake water is kept at a consistently high level. The whole scene is described as 'one of the most truly tranquil and beautiful garden scenes in China.'[139]

The writer visited this garden in the spring of 1983, and was impressed by the consummate care which had been given to the smallest details of the design. The original southern entrance, which led into the sedan chair hall has now become part of the city street, but the beautiful brick-built doorway with its carvings of scenes of court life is still intact. Brick-carving was an ancient craft in China and some excellent examples can be seen in some museums. An interesting feature of this entrance is the high step which signifies the high rank of the owner of the house. Today, access to the garden is via the former rear entrance in the north. A plain passage terminates in a bend to the right, and the visitor is immediately delayed by the arresting beauty of a small courtyard. It is glimpsed first through some elegantly carved doors, which occupy the whole length of one of the walls. A fine rock forms the centre of a design of rocks, trees, and plants against a white wall, while the pebble paving is in pink and grey, blending with the grey of the rocks. This is followed by a series of courtyards, in one of which a tumbled pile of rocks hides the steps to the door of an upstairs library. The Chinese regarded staircases as unsightly, and concealed them whenever possible. A large sophora japonica sends its branches above a corner of this courtyard,

[139]Ibid. p116.

where a wall, broken by ornamental lattices, partially hides the view beyond. Over the wall, and through the lattices can be seen the roof of a waterside *ting*. Although the lake is not visible, one becomes aware of a change of light as rippled reflections of the water play on the roof of the *ting* inviting the visitor to explore further. It is impossible to hurry round such a garden, as one delightful view or composition follows another, compelling attention. A guide or plan is surely needed if a way out is to be found! These are indeed enchanted gardens. In the words of the old Suzhou poet quoted above 'if one is to attain to an inner communion with the soul of the garden' one should relax, and submit oneself to it, as to a symphony or a work of art, and become temporarily spell-bound in another world, as was the fisherman in the tale of the Peach Blossom Spring. A classic Chinese garden is in every sense a work of art.

9

NORTH AND SOUTH
Contrasting Environments

Turning to atlas maps of China, it becomes clear that the main physical features tend to run on east-west lines. The three main rivers Huanghe, Changjiang and Xijiang, their basins bounded by mountain ranges, all follow this trend, though south of the Changjiang the direction is often north-east south-west. The result has been an age-long difficulty in north-south communication, mitigated somewhat on the eastern side by the Great Plain, stretching from Beijing to the mouth of the Changjiang. The Grand Canal has used this lowland for centuries, enabling contact between North and Central China.

Whereas North China, one of the cradles of Chinese civilization, was open to the north and west, and thence to the civilizations of Central Asia, the Middle East, and even the Roman Empire in Han times, Central and South China were hemmed in by the massive plateau of Tibet and the great ranges running south from the Himalaya to Indo-China.

The physical structure has affected the climate of China in many ways. A glance at climatic maps, brings out the importance of two 'lines': the 375mm annual rainfall line (isohyet) and the 0°C isotherm (equal temperature) line for January. 375 mm of rain can be said to mark approximately the ancient boundary between the possibility of agriculture, and the necessity of a nomadic lifestyle, the 'Steppe' and the 'Sown', entailing centuries of conflict between drought-stricken nomads and settled farmers. In the 1920s geography students were familiar with a book by an American, Ellsworth Huntington, called the *Pulse of Asia*, in which the writer sought to correlate periods of drought in Central Asia with invasions of the more 'settled' lands of Europe and Asia by such 'barbarians' as Goths, Huns, Magyars, Tartars and Mongols, the drying out of Central Asia causing periodic surges of nomadic herders towards better watered lands. Though some of his conclusions were far-fetched, they contained an element of truth. At one time it was even suggested that the Great Wall of China was indirectly responsible for the fall of the Roman Empire, as the frustrated nomads fell back, and started a chain reaction of westward movements!

The 0°C isotherm for January runs south of the Shandong peninsula and the Huanghe marking off the Northern Great Plain and the fertile loess lands of the earliest Chinese civilization as the region of harshest winters, characterized by frozen rivers and lakes, and bitter north-west winds, often dust-laden from the Gobi Desert. However, in spring temperatures rise steeply to a hot summer during which most of the 375mm of the annual rainfall occurs. It is interesting to note that the latitude of Beijing, 40° north of the Equator, is the same as that of Rome, Madrid, and New York, the severe winters being the result of Beijing's position on the eastern side of the great cold land mass of Siberia. Further south in the Changjiang valley, other anomalies occur. The river mouth of the great port of Shanghai can experience bitter north-west winds in winter, while the rest of the great valley is protected by mountains and in the far west province of Sichuan temperatures in January are equivalent to those in Cornwall, 6–7°C giving a winter virtually frost free, though more than 2500km inland, but sheltered by surrounding mountains.

The lush green landscape of South China, sometimes called the 'land of multiple harvests', with winter temperatures between 10° and 20°C and ample rainfall, is a complete contrast to the dry North with its bitter winters, where irrigation has always been essential to agriculture, and it is sometimes difficult to reap one successful harvest in a year. Life in the South has been generally more carefree and easygoing, and the cities less rigidly planned than those of the North. It must be remembered, however, that the whole of

‘China Proper’ lies south of latitude 40°N, and therefore enjoys hot summers. The cold winters are shorter and sunnier than those in Europe, Asia, and North America, in higher latitudes.

China has the longest history of continuous civilization of any country in the world. The origin of some of the written characters used today can be seen in the ‘oracle bone’ inscriptions of 5000 years ago. Attempts at conquest by nomadic peoples from the North and West, although sometimes temporarily successful, seem in the end to have been absorbed and finally led to the sinicization of the invaders. Today’s huge population of over a billion people consists of 93 per cent of Han Chinese and 7 per cent of ethnic minorities. These include four million Manchus and three million Mongols, to mention only the more successful invaders of the past: 55 nationalities altogether of which 20 number fewer than 50,000. Others are Zhuang 13 million, Hui 7 million, Uygur 6 million, Yi and Miao 5 million each and Tibetans 2 million. Strangely enough, this 7 per cent occupies 60 per cent of Chinese land,[140] in other words the least productive areas of mountain and desert which constitute the borders of China. The population is centred on the Great Plain, the Changjiang valley, and the coastal areas, and China has achieved the considerable feat of feeding a billion people on the 21 per cent of the land which is cultivable.

There is a legend that the first Emperor of a unified China, Shihuangdi, made a journey to the moon on a magic carpet to survey his empire in preparation for building a wall round it to secure its frontiers. He had intended to make it U-shaped, opening towards the ocean on the east, but noticing that there appeared to be an effective barrier of mountains and desert to the south and west and not much threat from the ocean he decided that the north was the most vulnerable and planned his wall accordingly. In fact numbers of small stretches of wall had already been built by the so-called Warring States. Shihuangdi consolidated these into the first continuous wall. It

[140] *The Contemporary Atlas of China*, London: Weidenfeld and Nicholson, 1988, p98.

was to become part of Chinese history, the '10,000-*li* rampart' (1 *li* = 0.5km). Hundreds of thousands of conscript workers died in its construction. The legend of the young widow, Meng Jiangnu, has been handed down from the early days. Her young husband, a scholar, whose political views were unacceptable to the authorities was sentenced to forced labour on the Wall. With many others, he died, and his body was built into the Wall. His wife had dreamed that he had asked her to bring some winter clothes. She made some and set off on the difficult journey. Arriving at last, with the help of an 'immortal' disguised as an old woman, she was told that he had died, and she wept for three days and nights. The gods heard her, and caused the Wall to split in a place revealing piles of bones. Among them she saw a skeleton hand holding half a jade hairpin, and knew it must be her husband's, as they had broken the hairpin between them when they had parted. She collected his bones and set off home to give them proper burial, essential for the soul to rest in peace. Shihuangdi heard of her, and as she was very beautiful, ordered her to be a concubine. She dared not refuse, but managed to get permission for her husband's funeral to take place near the Eastern Sea. This was granted, and after the ceremony she threw herself into the sea. Shihuangdi was very impressed, and ordered a monument to be built for her.

The geographer Thomas Tregear notes that the main route of the Wall follows fairly closely the line of the 15 inch (375mm) isohyet (rainfall line) the important division already noted between the possibilities of a nomadic and pastoral life and of settled agriculture. This boundary was to worry the Chinese authorities for generations: the problem of keeping the Great Wall in repair, and garrisoning it adequately to prevent incessant harassing by nomads was to haunt dynasty after dynasty. In 157 BC the Han emperor Wendi was to die of grief over this problem, and the money involved in it. It proved impossible to keep the Wall in peak condition at all times, so again and again the steppe peoples broke through and some became settled farmers, or some of the farmers deserted in times of drought, and even joined the nomads. Much depended on the periodic rise of charismatic leaders among the steppe peoples. It was a cultural frontier as much as a physical one. To the north were the horse-riders, good bowmen, dressed in skins and with no learning; to the south they wore silk, wrote and read books, and engaged in agriculture.[141] From time to time thousands of settlers were 'planted' south of the Wall to ensure the spread of civilization.

The long persistence of the Imperial capital in the north of the country reflects not only the anxiety to hold the frontier, but the importance of the trade and cultural contacts via the Silk Road through Central Asia, with the main cradle area of Chinese civilization. From the ancient Shang dynasty capitals Anyang and Zhengzhou, through the long dominance of sites near present day Xi'an, (Xianyang of Shihuangdi and the splendour of Han and Tang Chang'an), to the 'eastern' capitals of Luoyang and Kaifeng, the so-called 'southern capital', Nanjing, came into use for only short periods, during the time of the Three Kingdoms and for short periods between 280 and 1368 AD. In spite of its name, Nanjing is actually in Central China, but was to be capital again when the Ming dynasty succeeded the Mongols in 1368, and then only for 34 years, and for 22 years from 1927 until 1949 under the Nationalist Government (the Guomindang). During the second World War Chongqing took over as capital for a time. The beautiful city of Hangzhou enjoyed over 50 years as capital of the Southern Song (1127–1280), but no city further south has ever served as Imperial capital. With the coming of the Mongols and the Yuan dynasty (1271–1368) the capital was moved to Cambaluc (Beijing) where it has remained ever since, except for several short periods already mentioned.

The Great Wall has been a symbol for 2000 years of the triumph of Chinese civilization over the nomadic peoples of the steppes. The Han dynasty used it as a base for control of the all-important trade routes westward, and as a deterrent to

---

[141] Jonathan Fryer, *The Great Wall of China*, London: Book Club Associates, 1975. Much of the section on the Great Wall is based on this.

the Xiongnu, a steppe people probably related to the Huns, who were a continuous threat to the North. During Han times the Wall was extended for 480km to the West, making a total length of almost 3200km. The great Han Emperor Wudi, who reigned for 54 years, organized an efficient system of watch towers and garrisons, the latter not only of conscripts. Some officers had their families with them and were allotted land and houses. There was a good system of communication between the watch towers. The arrangement of garrisons and watch towers turned out over the centuries to be a more important factor than the physical barrier of the wall itself. At one point in Han times, the chief of the Xiongnu offered his help in the management, but the Emperor Wudi wisely refused his offer!

Following the collapse of the Han, China entered one of its periods of disunity, and the Wall was neglected. In the 5th century it was repaired by a leader of the Toba tribe, invaders from the steppe who had resisted sinicization. From time to time would-be invaders fortified parts of the wall against each other. By the 6th century some stability had returned. The Sui dynasty came to power, and new stretches of the wall to about 480km east of the Huanghe were added. The 300 years of the Tang dynasty were free of trouble along the frontier, and the Wall was regarded as a monument to the past. The famous Tang poets often wrote of the hardships suffered by those who built the Wall, or fought to defend it. At this time the wall was secured against the main threat, which came from the Tibetans and Turks. However further to the north, future trouble was brewing with the rise of the Mongols.

The Northern Song dynasty (960–1126) was militarily weak, and after incursions by Tangut tribes from Tibet and Jurchens and Khitans from Manchuria the capital was moved from Kaifeng to Hangzhou in 1126 and the Southern Song dynasty took over. By 1215 northern China was falling to the Mongols and in 1260 Kublai Khan was established in Beijing, and governed a vast empire extending from Syria to China. The Mongols had difficulty in conquering South China, where the environment was strange to them and the Chinese fought fiercely. It was 1276 before Hangzhou finally fell.

In 1271 Kublai Khan had founded the Yuan dynasty, but it lasted only until 1368. The Mongols never assimilated, and in spite of the wonders of organization recorded by Marco Polo, the Chinese looked back on the Mongol period as one of the blackest in their history. The last Yuan emperor fled in 1368, and the Ming dynasty began, with its capital in Nanjing.

The Ming was the only regime to control the entire length of the Great Wall, which they rebuilt and repaired to the highest standard since Han times. The western sector was the frontier with the 'uncivilized'. In the east Chinese authority extended beyond the Wall, which was thought to be a sufficient delaying factor to give the army time to overcome any invader. Mongol raids were a nuisance in the early 15th century, but the strengthening and re-garrisoning of the Great Wall finally stopped them.[142]

The section of Wall seen by visitors today has its origins in Ming times, when the former structure of tamped earth was replaced by a core of earth, gravel, lime and brick, encased with stone or brick seven or eight layers thick. In the 16th century more renovations took place, when granite blocks 4m long, with stone drains every 15m were placed along the present wall. The average height of the Wall here is 6.6m, and the base is 4.5–7.5m thick. Every 180m there are towers 12–18m high and 9–12m square. The top is 4m wide. By the later years of the 16th century another nomad leader, this time of the Manchus, was rising in the north. In the 1550s he had established an empire from the sea to Tibet, but failed in an attempt to capture Beijing. For 20 years he threatened north China, where the old arguments raged at the court concerning the barbarian problem. The Wall only seemed to be effective when the nomads were weak; likewise Chinese offensive action against them. Could they be persuaded to settle?

It was at this time, the last quarter of the 16th and the first of the 17th century that the major Ming renovations of the Wall were undertaken, but once this was finished, a period of

---

[142]Ibid.

weaker government set in and the slow rise of the Manchus in the north-east was ignored, though they had captured Liaodong. They were a mixture of pastoral and agricultural people, descendants of the Nurchen. Many Chinese had settled in Manchuria in the Ming dynasty, but by the late 16th century Chinese influence was waning, and some of them withdrew to China. This led to an advance of the Manchus, and the new leader created the system of 'banners' to build up the army. At first, attempts to capture Chinese strongholds failed, and stalemate set in for about 20 years. Meanwhile the Ming government was becoming more corrupt and inefficient, leading to rebellion in north China. In a quarrel between the rebel leader and a Chinese general, the latter allied with the Manchus and the rebel leader was confronted by a big force of Manchu horsemen, and forced to flee. The last Ming emperor hanged himself, and finally the Qing dynasty was born. The Manchus controlled both sides of the Great Wall which was never to regain its former significance. However, it became a symbol of Chinese history, and as such achieved honour and world-wide publicity in 1969 when it turned out to be the only man-made object visible from the Moon. It is a 'must' for every tourist to China, as well as many of the Chinese themselves.

Perhaps the best way to appreciate the physical contrast between north and south China is to travel between Guangzhou, and Beijing in winter. The writer remembers three such occasions. In November 1976 the temperature in Guangzhou was 21°C. The countryside was green and gold, and a rice harvest was in full swing. Snow was reported in Beijing, but on arrival at the airport we were met not by snow, but by a biting northerly wind. During the next few days this was mitigated by brilliant sunshine. However on a trip to the Great Wall, we felt the full force of the wind in spite of the midday sun, and the party of 24 were issued with large padded greatcoats by the accompanying guides, who had warned us before departure from the hotel, to put on every item of warm clothing which we had with us. For most of us it was the coldest wind we had ever experienced: it stung our faces, probably because it contained minute particles of ice, a characteristic of winter winds in north China.

The second occasion was in late winter, in April 1983. Temperatures were higher, but the north was bone dry. Descending to Beijing airport, and later on a train to Chengde, north of the Great Wall, we saw an immaculate landscape-in-waiting, the yellow-grey earth bare of crops but meticulously prepared for the spring rain and planting time: boundaries repaired, channels dug for irrigation, fruit trees surrounded by small hollows to catch the rain, the earth finely tilled. Later we travelled south, where spring flowers were in full bloom, but the air was damp and misty, and the early rain had already begun. A spectacular thunderstorm accompanied the train from Shanghai to Guangzhou.

The third example was over a shorter distance from Xi'an to Changsha in late November 1976 by air. After five days in Xi'an mantled by a dust smog preventing a hoped-for view of the Tian Shan mountains we took off in the fog and headed south. Gradually the fog thinned, and broke into long streamers which appeared to be travelling with us until they fell away. As we approached the Changjiang valley, a sunlit landscape appeared below, brightly coloured in red, green and blue: red earth, green vegetation and crops, blue irrigation ponds strung along the valleys like beads. After five days of grey-yellow smog the green appeared unusually brilliant: to parody a well known advertisement for washing powder, we all said we had never seen such 'greenness'.

The winter landscape brings out the contrast between the rocks and soil of north and south. The Great Plain consists of sediments deposited by the Huanghe. In summer it is a patchwork of crops, but the bare soil of winter reveals a mixture of loess and alluvium, broken here and there by sudden hills of basic rock. Further inland the predominate yellow of windblown loess prevails.

The characteristics of the Southern landscape are quite different. There is much red soil in the Changjiang Basin, but further south the scenery is dominated by limestone. The whole area, in company with the Himalayas has been rising steadily for thousands of years, and the ample rainfall has carved the rock into fantastic scenery to which geologists have given the name 'karst', after similar features studied in Croatia and Bosnia. The action of water made slightly acidic by decaying vegetation, is to dissolve the limestone, often along joint planes producing underground streams and lakes, extensive caves with stalactites and stalagmites, and the strange 'spires' or 'towers', pointed mountains reminiscent of Chinese paintings, which characterise the Guilin area and Lijiang river basin, now a favourite tourist region.

To the south-west in Yunnan, an area of smaller limestone 'spires' is known as the 'Stone Forest'. As a result of millennia of uplift some of the limestone 'towers' near Guilin have caves at several levels representing past water tables, the higher ones now being completely dry. Sometimes they form a tunnel through the mountain. The writer saw a number of these laid out with tables and chairs occupied by retired men playing mahjong and various card games. Tea and light refreshments were available, and the caves were cool and airy. A member of the party asked about retired women, and the guide explained that they retire earlier, at the age of 50, to enable them to look after their grand-children, so that both parents can work. We had noticed that in some of the parks and gardens, the tea-houses were occupied exclusively by elderly men.

The higher levels of the 'towers' afford fine views across the landscape, but this is best seen from the air. Apart from crops, it is uniformly green, the bare limestone coated with low shrubs and plants which give the mountains a strange furry appearance. As well as the pointed mountains, there are areas of rounded limestone, protuberances all much the same height, appearing from the air to resemble a type of rubber or plastic doormat. The flat land between the limestone hills is a brilliant patchwork of cultivation. The warmth and plentiful rainfall of South China enables almost continuous cropping. A boat trip along the Lijiang is like a journey in a Chinese painting, or the unrolling of a silk scroll. Along the river bank giant bamboos bend over the water, their arching stems and dense small leaves resembling Prince-of-Wales feathers. Behind them rise the fantastic outlines of the limestone 'towers'. On the river great family junks ply back and forth. They are the homes of river dwellers who make a living from fishing and the transport of goods. A close-up view reveals a cabin open but roofed at the stern end, with tables and chairs, live chickens in cages, small containers with growing vegetables, a line of washing, and toddlers peeping over the rims of barrels, or secured from falling overboard by a rope round the waist. The breeding of cormorants used for fishing is a traditional skill handed down from father to son, and sometimes cages housing these special birds can be seen. A bamboo fishing raft, made by lashing together several long bamboos, may be strapped along the side of the junk together with items such as a ladder, spare shoulder-poles and steering oars, ropes and baskets, and the wide picturesque hats worn by the river people. Not an inch of space is wasted. The junk is a masterpiece in the use of limited space and also evidence of the marvellous versatility of bamboo, which helps to explain the description of China as a 'vegetable civilization'.

Traditionally South China had few roads. Communication was by water, or paths about one metre wide, sometimes paved with stone slabs, sometimes just ridges between rice fields. These were adequate for the usual means of transport by shoulder-pole and baskets, or by wheelbarrow, a Chinese invention. This came in various forms from the large strong family version, with a central axis and a long shelf each side, which could carry the family and produce to market, to the smaller push and pull varieties which can still be seen even on the new roads in the South, and in remoter areas. The writer saw a number still in use south of the Changjiang in 1976. The man pushing or pulling was wearing a yoke across his shoulders and the back of his neck. From this yoke two ropes came down and were attached to the handles of the wheelbarrow. The writer photographed one example where a man was pushing one wheelbarrow and pulling another at the same time, both being attached to his yoke, and the handles linked. These interesting devices are obviously being superseded by the all-purpose bicycle, which can be piled with baskets back and front leaving just enough room for the rider, and can be used on narrow paths. Lighter loads are still carried on the ubiquitous shoulder-pole, and the eight-horsepower tractor, referred to earlier, can be seen everywhere, 'harnessed' to small carts, wherever a road is available.

There are as many views of China as there are viewers. Although it has been possible since the mid-sixties to choose to study China in some A-level Geography syllabuses there is almost a complete lack of Chinese studies in schools generally. For adults perception depends largely on opportunity; for reading, for contact with experienced 'old China hands', or Chinese students studying in Britain, or for travel to China. The whole field is so vast, covering every aspect of human activity in an area of great scenic and climatic variety that only a 'Renaissance man' like Joseph Needham with his magnum opus *Science and Civilization in China* can begin to cover the ground adequately. For the rest of us, fascination with Chinese civilization and its contribution to mankind becomes a personal treasure hunt: a visit to an exhibition, a good book, an informed trip to China; these all contribute to a box of delights in which we can rummage happily for years, always remembering the vast *terra incognita* for which we cannot find time. We turn in gratitude to those fortunate or clever enough to spend a lifetime in the study of Chinese language and literature, such as Arthur Waley and others who through their sensitive translations have brought the beauty of the splendid Tang poetry within reach of those whose mother tongue is English. Others have done the same for Chinese art and philosophy, and for exquisite craftsmanship in porcelain and silk. We have a saying 'The Greeks had a word for it.' Perhaps we should add another; 'The Chinese saw, made, invented, ... this, many years before it reached the West' in acknowledgement of the many Chinese 'firsts'.

The modern sinophile watches with some apprehension as the impact of so-called 'Western' values blows away many of the old Chinese stabilities: as the peasants desert the land, nurtured so carefully for thousands of years. As a Chinese student said to the writer 'Now it is nothing but money,

money, money.' Things may fall apart but we must hope, that as for past millennia, the centre will hold, and the lessons learned will not be forgotten: that the best of the past will survive this latest trauma. The kaleidoscope is still shaking, but when the pieces finally fall into place, the new China will surely be more mature, and will have emerged finally from her old isolation to take her rightful place as a leader and major contributor to the life of man on this planet.

CHRONOLOGY

Summary of Main Events in Chinese History

Period		Events
BC5000–1520 Prehistoric and Legendary	*Disunity and Feudalism*	Neolithic culture. Villages. Textiles. Millet grown. Rice grown (c.5000 BC). Silk (c.4800 BC). Yangshao pottery. Oracle bones.
BC1520–1030 SHANG kingdom		Bronze vessels. Weaving. Painting. Music. Capital: Anyang. Land communal.
BC1030–480 ZHOU dynasty (Feudal Age)		BC551–479 Confucius. Capitals: Chang'an and Luoyang. Iron began to oust bronze. Dyke building. BC771–476 Spring and Autumn Period.
BC480–221 'Warring States'		BC500–200 'Golden Age' of Philosophy. BC350–300 Laozi. BC372–289 Mencius. Li Bing – irrigation in Sichuan.
BC221–207 QIN dynasty	*First unification*	Private ownership of land. End of feudalism. First empire under Qin Shihuangdi. The Great Wall. Village government. Careers open to talent. Capital: Xianyang.
BC206–AD220 HAN dynasty		Silk trade. Capital: Luoyang and Chang'an. Contacts with Rome. Paper invented. AD58–75 Buddhist priests from India. Secret of silk smuggled out.
AD220–265 The THREE KINGDOMS	*Disunity*	Control of Tarim Basin lost. Three capitals: Luoyang, Chengdu, Nanjing. AD233 Mariners' compass invented. Sea traffic increased.

Period		Events
AD265–317 JIN dynasty	*Unity*	AD300 Arab traders in Guangzhou. Migration of Han people to South and South West. AD300 floods and drought.
AD317–420 Barbarian invasions AD420–589 Northern and Southern dynasties	*'Panic'* *Disunity*	AD386–535 Buddhist and Indian influence: Monks made progress with irrigation, drainage, flood prevention and canals. Yunnan trade route blocked by Tibetans. Invasion from North and West.
AD589–618 SUI dynasty		Grand Canal built. Buddhism widespread.
AD618–906 TANG dynasty	*Unity*	Great expansion. 'Farm colonies' in South (military). Trade with Persia, Arabs and with Japan and Korea. Public examinations for Civil Service. AD751 Turkestan lost to Islam.
AD907–960 Five 'little dynasties'	*Disunity (partial)*	8th–13th centuries: growth of cities and merchants; development of mathematics and the arts. New crops, rotation of crops: manuring, irrigation machinery.
AD960–1279 SONG (North and South) dynasty	*'Panic'* *Unity* *Disunity (partial)*	Completion of conquest of the South. Printing, painting and ceramics reached all-time high. Foot binding. Capital: Hangzhou.
AD1279–1368 YUAN dynasty	*Unity*	Kublai Khan. Marco Polo in China. Much trade along 'Silk Road' and coastal shipping. Silk, porcelain, tea and camphor exported. Capital: Beijing (Cambaluc)
AD1368–1644 MING dynasty		Great expansion. First Jesuit missionaries arrived. Grand Canal fell into disuse. AD1557 Portuguese sailors in Macao. Fine porcelain. Expeditions to Indian Ocean and Africa.

Period		Events
AD1644–1911 QING dynasty	*Unity*	Increasing reluctant contact with the West. AD1661–1722 Kangxi emperor. Examinations standardized: marked by calligraphy only! AD1736–96 splendid period under Emperor Qianlong. AD1742 Pope condemned Jesuits' attempted integration of Christianity and Confucianism. Cao Xueqin's *A Dream of Red Mansions*. AD1793 Lord Macartney audience with emperor. AD1839–41 Opium War. Loss of Hong Kong.
AD1850–1950 A century of disaster	*Disinte-gration*	1851–64 Taiping rebellion. 1858–60 Treaties opened ports to Western trade. 1880s Loss of tributary states in Indo-China. Russia in Xinjiang. 1894–5 Sino-Japanese War. 1900 Boxer rebellion. 1912 Republic. Sun Yat-Sen (1866–1925)
		1915 Japan's 21 demands. 1919–26 Warlords, civil war. 1928–34 Civil war: Communists v. Nationalists. 1931 Japanese invasion of Manchuria. 1934–5 The Long March. 1937 Guomindang (Nationalists) and Communists unite v. Japan. 1937–45 War with Japan. 1945 Japanese surrender 1947–9 Civil War: Guomindang v. Communists. 1949 Retreat of Chiang Kai-Shek and government to Formosa.

Period		Events
AD1949 to present day	*Unity*	People's Republic established. Mao Zedong. Chairman of Communist Party 1949–76; Zhou Enlai, Prime Minister 1949–76. 1950–2 Land Reform. 1950–3 Korean War. 1953–7 First 5-year plan. Soviet aid on industrial projects. 1954 Constitution. 1955–7 Collectivization of agriculture. 1958 Communes and Great Leap Forward. 1959–61 Droughts and floods. Setback. 1960–4 Quarrel with USSR. 1962–4 Economic recovery. 1963 Agreement with Pakistan. 1964 Recognition by France. First atomic bomb. 1966 Cultural revolution.
	Open Door Policy	1971 (October) China takes seat at the UN. 1972 President Nixon visits China. 1975 Revised constitution. 1976 Deaths of Mao Zedong and Zhou Enlai. Election of Chairman Hua Guofeng. Overthrow of the 'Gang of Four'. Tiananmen incident (April). Tangshan earthquake (July). 1977 Deng Xiaoping rehabilitated. New 'Open-door' policy. 1978 Chairman Hua tours abroad. 1979 Campaign for 'The Four Modernizations'. Stricter discipline imposed. 'Democracy Wall'. 1980 New legal system. 1981 Responsibility System. Hua Guofeng replaced by Hu Yaobang.

Period		Events
		1980–5 Special Economic Zones and Open Cities on east coast. 1984 Deng Xiaoping signs agreement with Britain on the future of Hong Kong. 1986 Reform of political structure proposed by scholars: student demonstrations result in dismissal of Hu Yaobang. 1987 Zhao Ziyang replaces Hu Yaobang. 1988 Li Peng premier. 1987–8 Tibet: demonstrations suppressed by force. 1989 (April): Student demonstrations for democracy. Zhao Ziyang dismissed. (4th June) Massacre in Tiananmen Square. 1990 4th census: population 1,134 million. 1991 Severe floods in Anhui and Jiangsu provinces. Jiang Qing (Mao's widow) commits suicide. 1992 Construction of Three Gorges dam on Yangtze approved. 1994 Increasing unrest due to unemployment in rural areas. Two underground nuclear tests. 1995 More underground nuclear tests. 1997 Death of Deng Xiaoping. Huanghe fails nine times to reach Bohai Gulf, causing grave problems with water supply. Building of the Three Gorges dam begins. Hong Kong reverts to China.

PARTIAL BIBLIOGRAPHY

General Reading

Birch, Cyril. *Anthology of Chinese Literature*, Harmondsworth: Penguin, 1967.

Bonavia, David. *The Chinese: A Portrait*, London: Allen Lane, 1981.

Dawson, Raymond. *The Chinese Experience*, London: Weidenfeld and Nicholson, 1978.

Han Suyin. *The Crippled Tree*, London: Jonathan Cape, 1965.

Spence, Jonathan D. *The Gate of Heavenly Peace: The Chinese and their Revolution 1895–1980*, Harmondsworth: Penguin, 1983.

Spence, Jonathan D. *The Search for Modern China*, London: Hutchinson, 1990.

Zhang Xinxin and Sang Ye. *Chinese Lives*, London: Macmillan, 1987.

Recent Events

Benewick, Robert and Wingrove, Paul. *Reforming the Revolution: China in Transition*. Basingstoke: Macmillan Education, 1988.

Cottrell, Robert. *Tiananmen: The Rape of Peking*, London: The Independent and Doubleday, 1989.

Wright, Elizabeth. *The Chinese People Stand Up*, London: BBC Books, 1989.

Geography

Cannon, Terry and Jenkins, Alan. *The Geography of Contemporary China*, London: Routledge, 1990.

Cotterell, Yong Yap and Arthur. *Chinese Civilization*, London: Weidenfeld and Nicholson, 1977.

Money, D.C. *China: The Land and the People*, London: Evan Bros., 1984.

History

Andersson, Johan Gunnar. *Children of the Yellow Earth*, Cambridge, Mass: MIT Press, 1973.

Cameron, Nigel. *Barbarians and Mandarins: Thirteen Centuries of Western Travellers in China*, New York: Weatherhill, 1970.

Dawson, Raymond. *Imperial China*, London: Hutchinson, 1972.

Dawson, Raymond. *Legacy of China*, Oxford: Clarendon Press, 1964.

Gernet, Jacques. *A History of Chinese Civilization*, trans. R. Foster. Cambridge: CUP, 1982.

Gittings, John. *China Changes Face*, Oxford: OUP, 1989.

Hinton, William. *Fanshen*, Harmondsworth: Penguin, 1972.

Hinton, William. *Shenfan*, London: Picador, 1983.

King, F.H. *Farmers of Forty Centuries*, Emmaus, Pa: Rodale Press, 1973.

Needham, Joseph. *Science and Civilization in China*, Vol 1, Cambridge: CUP, 1954.

Polo, M. *The Travels of Marco Polo*, trans. R.E. Latham, (Penguin Classics), Harmondsworth: Penguin, 1958.

Rawson, J. *Ancient China: Art and Archaeology*, London: British Museum, 1980.

Ronan, Colin A. *The Shorter Science and Civilization in China*, (Abridgement of Joseph Needham), Vol II. Cambridge: CUP, 1981.

Snow, Edgar. *Red China Today: The Other Side of the River*, Harmondsworth: Penguin, 1970.

Snow, Edgar. *Red Star over China*, Harmondsworth: Penguin, 1972.

Tuan Yi-Fu. *China*, (Vol 1 of The World's Landscapes), Harlow: Longmans, 1970.

Watson, William. *Early Civilisation in China*, London: Thames and Hudson, 1966.

Art, Poetry etc.

Boyd, Andrew. *Chinese Architecture and Town Planning 1500 BC–AD 1911*, London: Tiranti, 1962.

Cahill, James. *Chinese Painting*, (Treasures of Asia Series), London: A. Skira Macmillan, 1977.

Chang, K.C. *The Archaeology of Ancient China*, New Haven: Yale University Press, 1959.

Cooper, Arthur. *The Deep Woods' Business*, London: Wellsweep, 1990.

Cooper, Arthur. *Li Po and Tu Fu*, (Penguin Classics), Harmondsworth: Penguin, 1973.

Graham, A.C. *Poems of the Late Tang*, (Penguin Classics), Harmondsworth: Penguin, 1965.

Graham, A.C. *Poems of the West Lake*, London: Wellsweep, 1990.

Hawkes, David. *The Songs of the South*, (Penguin Classics), Harmondsworth: Penguin, 1985.

Johnston, R. Stewart. *Scholar Gardens of China,* Cambridge: CUP, 1991.

Keswick, Maggie. *The Chinese Garden*, London: Academy Editions, 1978.

Lao Tzu. *Tao te Ching*, trans. D.C. Lau, Book One, XXV, (Penguin Classics), Harmondsworth: Penguin, 1968.

Loehr, Max. *The Great Painters of China*, Oxford: Phaidon, 1980.

Robinson, G.W. *Poems of Wang Wei*, (Penguin Classics), Harmondsworth: Penguin, 1973.

Sickman, Laurence and Soper, Alexander. *The Art and Architecture of China*, (Pelican History of Art), Harmondsworth: Penguin, 1971.

Sullivan, Michael. *The Birth of Landscape Painting in China*, London: Routledge and Kegan Paul, 1962.

Tregear, Mary. *Chinese Art*, London: Thames and Hudson, 1980.

van Over, Raymond. *I Ching (Book of Changes)*, London: New English Library, 1971.

Waley, Arthur. *Analects of Confucius*, London: Unwin Hyman, 1988.

Waley, Arthur. *Book of Songs*, London: George Allen and Unwin, 1969.

Waley, Arthur. *Chinese Poems*, London: George Allen and Unwin, 1961.

Waley, Arthur. *Life and Times of Po Chü-i*, London: George Allen and Unwin, 1970.

Waley, Arthur. *The Poetry and Career of Li Po*, London: George Allen and Unwin, 1950.

GLOSSARY OF OLD AND NEW SPELLINGS

The following is a list of names etc. mentioned in the text with their Pinyin and former equivalent spellings. The first section shows Wade-Giles spellings (or those used by other, older romanizing systems) into Pinyin; the second section shows Pinyin spellings and their former spellings using Wade-Giles or other, older systems.

Wade-Giles or other	Pinyin
An Lan	An Lan
An-yang	Anyang
Canton	Guangzhou
Chang Ch'ien	Zhang Qian
Ch'ang-an	Chang'an
Ch'ang-sha	Changsha
Ch'ên Hung-shou	Chen Hongshou
Ch'ên Yün	Chen Yun
Chên-hai	Zhenhai
Chêng Ho	Zheng He
Chêng Kuo	Zheng Guo
Chêng-chou	Zhengzhou
Ch'êng-tê	Chengde
Ch'êng-tu	Chengdu
Chhin	Qin
ch'i	qi
Chia	Jia
Chia Tao	Jia Dao
Chia-ch'ing	Jiaqing
Chia-ling	Jialing
Chiang	Jiang
Chiang Ch'ing	Jiang Qing
Chiang Kai-Shek	Jiang Jieshi (Jiang Zhongzheng)
Ch'ien Lung	Qianlong
Ch'ien-t'ing	Qianting
Ch'in	Qin
Chin-ch'êng	Jincheng
Chin-sha-chiang	Jinshajiang

Ch'ing	Qing
Ching-chiang	Jingjiang
Ching-tê-Chên	Jingdezhen
Ch'iu Chih-hai	Qiu Zhihai
Chiu-ch'üan	Jiuquan
Chou	Zhou
Chou Ch'ên	Zhou Chen
Chou Ên-lai	Zhou Enlai
Ch'u	Chu
Chu Chiang	Zhu Jiang
Chü Sung	Ju Song
Ch'u tz'ŭ	Chu Ci
Ch'ü Yüan	Qu Yuan
Chu-ko Liang	Zhuge Liang
Ch'ü-t'ang	Qutang
Chuang	Zhuang
Chuang Tzŭ	Zhuangzi
Chung-chou	Zhongzhou
Chung-shan	Zhongshan
Chungking	Chongqing
Ê-mei	Emei
fêng-shui	feng-shui
Fêng-Tu	Fengdu
Fouchou	Fuzhou
Fu-ling	Fuling
Hami	Hami
Han	Han
Han-yang	Hanyang
Hangchow	Hangzhou
Hankow	Hankou
Heilungkiang	Heilongjiang
Hêng	Heng
Honan	Henan
hong	hong
Hsi-chiang	Xijiang
Hsi-ling	Xiling
Hsieh	Xie
Hsieh Ling-yün	Xie Lingyun
Hsien-yang	Xianyang
Hsiung-nu	Xiongnu
Hsüan Tsang	Xuan Zang
Hsüan Tsung	Xuanzong
Hsüan-Ch'êng	Xuancheng
Hua	Hua
Hua Kuo-fêng	Hua Guofeng

Hua-Ch'ing	Huaqing
Hua-yüan-k'ou	Huayuankou
Huai	Huai
Hui	Hui
Hui Tsung	Huizong
Hunan	Hunan
Hung-wu	Hongwu
Hwang Ho	Huanghe
I	Yi
I-Ching	Yi Jing
Ichang	Yichang
Ipin	Yibin
Jehol	Chengde
Kaifeng	Kaifeng
Kanchow	Ganzhou
k'ang	kang
K'ang Hsi	Kangxi
Kansu	Gansu
K'ao-liang	Kaoliang
Kê-chou-pa	Gezhouba
Kiang-ling	Jiangling
Kirin	Jilin
Kowloon	Jiulong
Kuan-hsien	Guanxian
Kuanyin	Guanyin
Kuei	Gui
Kung-sun Shu	Gongsun Shu
Kunming	Kunming
Kuo Hsi	Guo Xi
Kuomintang	Guomindang
Kweilin	Guilin
Lan-t'ien	Lantian
Lanchow	Lanzhou
laodah	laoda
Li Êrh-lang	Li Erlang
Li Kiang	Lijiang
Li Ping	Li Bing
Li Po	Li Bai
Li-tui	Lidui
Liao-tung	Liaodong
Liu Chia	Liujia
Liu Pei	Liu Bei
Lo City	Luoyang
Loyang	Luoyang
Lu-p'an	Lupan

Lung-ch'üan	Longquan
Lung-shan	Longshan
Lung-yang	Longyang
Ma-wang-tui	Mawangdui
Mang-shan	Mangshan
Mao Tse-tung	Mao Zedong
Mei-chia-wu	Meijiawu
Mêng Chiang-nu	Meng Jiangnu
Mêng-liang	Mengliang
Mi Fu	Mi Fu
Mi-lou	Milou
Miao	Miao
Ming-huang	Minghuang
Minya Konka	Minya Gongga
Nan-yang	Nanyang
Nanking	Nanjing
Ningsia	Ningxia
Pa	Ba
Pa-T'ang	Batang
Pa-Tung	Badong
Pai Ti	Baidi
Pai-yü	Baiyu
p'ailou	pailou
Pan-p'o	Banpo
Pao-dou	Baotou
Pao-p'ing-k'ou	Baopingkou
Pei-hai	Beihai
Pei-lin	Beilin
Pei-Pei	Beibei
Peking	Beijing
P'êng Hsien	Peng Xian
Po Chü-i	Bai Juyi
Po-yang	Boyang
San-tou-p'ing	Sandouping
Sha-szu	Shasi
Shan-lin	Shanlin
shan-shui	shanshui
Shang	Shang
Shansi	Shanxi
Shantung	Shandong
Shensi	Shaanxi
Shigatse	Xigazê
Shih Ching	Shi Jing
Shih Huang Ti	Qinshihuang
Shih Huang Ti	Shihuangdi

Shu	Shu
Sian	Xi'an
Ssu-ma Kuang	Sima Guang
Suchow	Suzhou
Sun Ch'üan	Sun Quan
Sun Yat-Sen	Sun Yixian (Sun Zhongshan)
Sung	Song
Szechuan	Sichuan
Ta Ming Kung	Daminggong
Ta Shou	Da Shou
T'ai Hu	Taihu
T'ai Tsung	Tai Zong
T'ai-chi-ch'üan	Taijiquan
T'ai-T'ien	Tai Tian
T'ang	Tang
T'ang-shan	Tangshan
T'ao Ch'ien	Tao Qian (Tao Yuanming)
T'ao Yüan-ming	Tao Yuanming (Tao Qian)
Tao-tê-Ching	Daodejing
Taoism	Daoism
Têng Hsiao-p'ing	Deng Xiaoping
T'ien Wên	Tian Wen
T'ien-an-mên	Tiananmen
Ting	Ding
t'ing	ting
Ts'ang-Lang	Canglang
Ts'ao Hsüeh-ch'in	Cao Xueqin
Ts'ao Ts'ao	Cao Cao
Tsinghai	Qinghai
Ts'ung	Cong
tsung-tzŭ	zongzi
Tu Fu	Du Fu
Tu Mu	Du Mu
Tu-chiang-yen	Dujiangyan
T'ung-kuan	Tongguan
Tung-T'ing	Dongting
Tz'ŭ Hsi	Ci Xi
Tzŭ-kui	Zigui
Urumchi	Ürümqi
Wan Li	Wanli
Wan-hsien	Wanxian
Wang Tsai	Wang Zai
Wei	Wei
Wei Ho	Weihe
Wên Ti	Wendi

Wên-hsiang	Wenxiang
Wu	Wu
Wu Kiang	Wujiang
Wu Ti	Wudi
Wu-han	Wuhan
Wu-shan	Wushan
Wuchang	Wuchang
Wusih	Wuxi
Yang Kuei Fei	Yang Guifei
Yang Shao	Yangshao
Yangtze	Changjiang
Yellow River	Huanghe
Yên-yü	Yanyu
Yenching	Yanjing
Yüan	Yuan
Yüan Ming Yüan	Yuan Ming Yuan
Yüan Yeh	Yuan Ye
Yüeh Ch'ih	Yue Chi
Yün-yang	Yunyang
Yunglo	Yongle
Yunnan	Yunnan

Pinyin	**Wade-Giles or other**
An Lan	*An Lan*
Anyang	*An-yang*
Ba	*Pa*
Badong	*Pa-Tung*
Bai Juyi	*Po Chü-i*
Baidi	*Pai Ti*
Baiyu	*Pai-yü*
Banpo	*Pan-p'o*
Baopingkou	*Pao-p'ing-k'ou*
Baotou	*Pao-dou*
Batang	*Pa-T'ang*
Beibei	*Pei-Pei*
Beihai	*Pei-hai*
Beijing	*Peking*
Beilin	*Pei-lin*
Boyang	*Po-yang*
Canglang	*Ts'ang-Lang*
Cao Cao	*Ts'ao Ts'ao*
Cao Xueqin	*Ts'ao Hsüeh-ch'in*
Chang'an	*Ch'ang-an*
Changjiang	*Yangtze*
Changsha	*Ch'ang-sha*

Chen Hongshou	*Ch'ên Hung-shou*
Chen Yun	*Ch'ên Yün*
Chengde	*Ch'êng-tê*
Chengde	*Jehol*
Chengdu	*Ch'êng-tu*
Chongqing	*Chungking*
Chu	*Ch'u*
Chu Ci	*Ch'u tz'ŭ*
Ci Xi	*Tz'ŭ Hsi*
Cong	*Ts'ung*
Da Shou	*Ta Shou*
Daminggong	*Ta Ming Kung*
Daodejing	*Tao-tê-Ching*
Daoism	*Taoism*
Deng Xiaoping	*Têng Hsiao-p'ing*
Ding	*Ting*
Dongting	*Tung-T'ing*
Du Fu	*Tu Fu*
Du Mu	*Tu Mu*
Dujiangyan	*Tu-chiang-yen*
Emei	*Ê-mei*
feng-shui	*fêng-shui*
Fengdu	*Fêng-Tu*
Fuling	*Fu-ling*
Fuzhou	*Fouchou*
Gansu	*Kansu*
Ganzhou	*Kanchow*
Gezhouba	*Kê-chou-pa*
Gongsun Shu	*Kung-sun Shu*
Guangzhou	*Canton*
Guanxian	*Kuan-hsien*
Guanyin	*Kuanyin*
Gui	*Kuei*
Guilin	*Kweilin*
Guo Xi	*Kuo Hsi*
Guomindang	*Kuomintang*
Hami	*Hami*
Han	*Han*
Hangzhou	*Hangchow*
Hankou	*Hankow*
Hanyang	*Han-yang*
Heilongjiang	*Heilungkiang*
Henan	*Honan*
Heng	*Hêng*
hong	*hong*

Hongwu	*Hung-wu*
Hua	*Hua*
Hua Guofeng	*Hua Kuo-fêng*
Huai	*Huai*
Huanghe	*Hwang Ho*
Huanghe	*Yellow River*
Huaqing	*Hua-Ch'ing*
Huayuankou	*Hua-yüan-k'ou*
Hui	*Hui*
Huizong	*Hui Tsung*
Hunan	*Hunan*
Jia	*Chia*
Jia Dao	*Chia Tao*
Jialing	*Chia-ling*
Jiang	*Chiang*
Jiang Jieshi (Jiang Zhongzheng)	*Chiang Kai-Shek*
Jiang Qing	*Chiang Ch'ing*
Jiangling	*Kiang-ling*
Jiaqing	*Chia-ch'ing*
Jilin	*Kirin*
Jincheng	*Chin-ch'êng*
Jingdezhen	*Ching-tê-Chên*
Jingjiang	*Ching-chiang*
Jinshajiang	*Chin-sha-chiang*
Jiulong	*Kowloon*
Jiuquan	*Chiu-ch'üan*
Ju Song	*Chü Sung*
Kaifeng	*Kaifeng*
kang	*k'ang*
Kangxi	*K'ang Hsi*
Kaoliang	*K'ao-liang*
Kunming	*Kunming*
Lantian	*Lan-t'ien*
Lanzhou	*Lanchow*
laoda	*laodah*
Li Bai	*Li Po*
Li Bing	*Li Ping*
Li Erlang	*Li Êrh-lang*
Liaodong	*Liao-tung*
Lidui	*Li-tui*
Lijiang	*Li Kiang*
Liu Bei	*Liu Pei*
Liujia	*Liu Chia*
Longquan	*Lung-ch'üan*
Longshan	*Lung-shan*

Longyang	*Lung-yang*
Luoyang	*Lo City*
Luoyang	*Loyang*
Lupan	*Lu-p'an*
Mangshan	*Mang-shan*
Mao Zedong	*Mao Tse-tung*
Mawangdui	*Ma-wang-tui*
Meijiawu	*Mei-chia-wu*
Meng Jiangnu	*Mêng Chiang-nu*
Mengliang	*Mêng-liang*
Mi Fu	*Mi Fu*
Miao	*Miao*
Milou	*Mi-lou*
Minghuang	*Ming-huang*
Minya Gongga	*Minya Konka*
Nanjing	*Nanking*
Nanyang	*Nan-yang*
Ningxia	*Ningsia*
pailou	*p'ailou*
Peng Xian	*P'êng Hsien*
qi	*ch'i*
Qianlong	*Ch'ien Lung*
Qianting	*Ch'ien-t'ing*
Qin	*Chhin*
Qin	*Ch'in*
Qing	*Ch'ing*
Qinghai	*Tsinghai*
Qinshihuang	*Shih Huang Ti*
Qiu Zhihai	*Ch'iu Chih-hai*
Qu Yuan	*Ch'ü Yüan*
Qutang	*Ch'ü-t'ang*
Sandouping	*San-tou-p'ing*
Shaanxi	*Shensi*
Shandong	*Shantung*
Shang	*Shang*
Shanlin	*Shan-lin*
shanshui	*shan-shui*
Shanxi	*Shansi*
Shasi	*Sha-szu*
Shi Jing	*Shih Ching*
Shihuangdi	*Shih Huang Ti*
Shu	*Shu*
Sichuan	*Szechuan*
Sima Guang	*Ssu-ma Kuang*
Song	*Sung*

Sun Quan	*Sun Ch'üan*
Sun Yixian (Sun Zhongshan)	*Sun Yat-Sen*
Suzhou	*Suchow*
Tai Tian	*T'ai-T'ien*
Tai Zong	*T'ai Tsung*
Taihu	*T'ai Hu*
Taijiquan	*T'ai-chi-ch'üan*
Tang	*T'ang*
Tangshan	*T'ang-shan*
Tao Qian (Tao Yuanming)	*T'ao Ch'ien*
Tao Yuanming (Tao Qian)	*T'ao Yüan-ming*
Tian Wen	*T'ien Wên*
Tiananmen	*T'ien-an-mên*
ting	*t'ing*
Tongguan	*T'ung-kuan*
Ürümqi	*Urumchi*
Wang Zai	*Wang Tsai*
Wanli	*Wan Li*
Wanxian	*Wan-hsien*
Wei	*Wei*
Weihe	*Wei Ho*
Wendi	*Wên Ti*
Wenxiang	*Wên-hsiang*
Wu	*Wu*
Wuchang	*Wuchang*
Wudi	*Wu Ti*
Wuhan	*Wu-han*
Wujiang	*Wu Kiang*
Wushan	*Wu-shan*
Wuxi	*Wusih*
Xi'an	*Sian*
Xianyang	*Hsien-yang*
Xie	*Hsieh*
Xie Lingyun	*Hsieh Ling-yün*
Xigazê	*Shigatse*
Xijiang	*Hsi-chiang*
Xiling	*Hsi-ling*
Xiongnu	*Hsiung-nu*
Xuan Zang	*Hsüan Tsang*
Xuancheng	*Hsüan-Ch'êng*
Xuanzong	*Hsüan Tsung*
Yang Guifei	*Yang Kuei Fei*
Yangshao	*Yang Shao*
Yanjing	*Yenching*
Yanyu	*Yên-yü*

Yi	*I*
Yi Jing	*I-Ching*
Yibin	*Ipin*
Yichang	*Ichang*
Yongle	*Yunglo*
Yuan	*Yüan*
Yuan Ming Yuan	*Yüan Ming Yüan*
Yuan Ye	*Yüan Yeh*
Yue Chi	*Yüeh Ch'ih*
Yunnan	*Yunnan*
Yunyang	*Yün-yang*
Zhang Qian	*Chang Ch'ien*
Zheng Guo	*Chêng Kuo*
Zheng He	*Chêng Ho*
Zhengzhou	*Chêng-chou*
Zhenhai	*Chên-hai*
Zhongshan	*Chung-shan*
Zhongzhou	*Chung-chou*
Zhou	*Chou*
Zhou Chen	*Chou Ch'ên*
Zhou Enlai	*Chou Ên-lai*
Zhu Jiang	*Chu Chiang*
Zhuang	*Chuang*
Zhuangzi	*Chuang Tzŭ*
Zhuge Liang	*Chu-ko Liang*
Zigui	*Tzŭ-kui*
zongzi	*tsung-tzŭ*

INDEX

References to the Plates section are in *italics*.